INTERNATIONAL REALITIES

INTERNATIONAL REALITIES

BY

PHILIP MARSHALL BROWN
PROFESSOR OF INTERNATIONAL LAW AT PRINCETON UNIVERSITY

Salus populi suprema lex esto
—Twelve Tables

Imperii virtus securitas
—Spinoza

NEW YORK
CHARLES SCRIBNER'S SONS
1917

Copyright, 1917, by
CHARLES SCRIBNER'S SONS

Published January, 1917

TO

GEORGE GRAFTON WILSON, Ph.D., LL.D.
STIMULATING TEACHER, COUNSELLOR
AND FRIEND

PREFACE

Realpolitik has been badly discredited because of its Prussian associations. It has naturally become identified with the Bismarckian policy of "Blood and Iron"—the policy which sought German unity at the expense of other nations. In its essence, however, *Realpolitik* simply means that national policies should be based, not on theories and abstractions, but on solid realities. The chief concern of statesmen should be the protection of the legitimate interests of the State. The supreme law of the State which they are bound to respect is "the security of the State." It does not follow that a policy of enlightened self-interest means the elimination of ethical standards and ideals from international relations. It may often mean, rather, their realization and safeguard. Ideals and generous instincts are to be reckoned among the great international realities, as well as unworthy motives of antagonism and aggression. Enlightened self-interest, interpreted as the application of the Golden Rule to the affairs of nations, will ignore none of these realities.

Understood in this sense, *Realpolitik* stands in favorable contrast with policy dominated by sentiment and emotion. An example of this sentimental brand of policy is to be found in the repeal of the Panama Tolls Act in 1914. This was a question which was at least open to discussion. It was peculiarly suited for Arbitration. A wave of emotion, however, swept over the country. The American people, in a spirit of almost morbid self-abasement, voluntarily surrendered a valuable privilege which, in the opinion of many high-minded men, was entirely within our rights.

A schoolmaster may find it good policy to appeal to the manhood and sense of honor of a boy by reposing absolute confidence in him. A nation cannot afford to act on any such principle. If it knows that another nation is intent on a policy of aggrandizement and aggression, it must immediately adopt precautionary measures of defense. There are not lacking men of prominence and influence, however, who would strip the country of its defenses in order to prove the purity of its own motives! This amazing attitude reminds one of the fate of the Delaware Indians, who were evilly inspired by their worst enemies, the Iroquois, to disarm

PREFACE ix

and become the mediator in the quarrels and wars of the Indian Nations. The result, as should clearly have been foreseen, was the utter ruin of the Delaware Nation.

It would seem as if no argument were needed to demonstrate that national policies must be devised and executed in full recognition of international realities. International Law as a genuine system of law cannot be based merely on philosophical abstractions. It has lately been subjected to "ordeal by battle," and has been badly discredited. It has been found to contain much that is spurious. It has failed to apply itself strictly to its true task of "regulating the *peaceful* relations of States." It has preached and moralized, when it should have been concerned with the definition and protection of national interests.

This is the explanation and the excuse for the present volume. Since the Great War began I have been conscious, with many others, of the urgent necessity of a thorough reconstruction of the law of nations in accordance with the big facts of international life. I have set myself the task of endeavoring to ascertain the fundamental values in international relations.

The method followed has been to select certain of the large problems of international relations and treat them as separate topics illustrating and elucidating some of the basic principles of International Law. This has involved, naturally, considerable repetition; but it has served the purpose of placing reiterated emphasis on essential truths. Though there has been diversity of subject-matter, there has been unity of purpose and method.

I am conscious of the inadequacy of this attempt to deal with questions of such immense import. It is evident that they demand thorough, intensive treatment. It has not been possible, however, nor has it seemed to me desirable, to attempt here to do much more than call attention to and emphasize the nature of these great international realities.

I realize that if this volume should receive any consideration, the points of view advanced will be subjected to considerable criticism. I shall feel that I have accomplished my purpose, however, if discussion shall have been provoked. It is only through earnest, wide discussion that we can undertake the constructive work required to make International Law an efficient instrument for world-peace.

I am glad of an opportunity to express my

obligation to the writings of James Lorimer, that most stimulating Scotch publicist. He may not be entitled to the rank of an authority on International Law, but he has hardly received the credit due as an original, forceful thinker. His *Institutes of the Law of Nations* is rich in just observations and striking suggestions. I have quoted him somewhat freely, not by way of an authority, but rather for his vigor of expression.

Certain of the chapters were originally prepared as addresses or articles for publication. I desire particularly to acknowledge the kind courtesy of the publishers of the *North American Review* in permitting the inclusion in this volume of the following articles: "The Dangers of Pacifism," July, 1915; "International Realities," April, 1916; "Ignominious Neutrality," August, 1916; and "Democracy and Diplomacy," November, 1916.

I desire to express my grateful appreciation of the most helpful criticism and suggestions of my colleague and friend, Professor Edward S. Corwin, in the preparation of this volume.

PHILIP MARSHALL BROWN.

12 September, 1916,
WILLIAMSTOWN, MASSACHUSETTS.

CONTENTS

PREFACE vii

CHAPTER I

INTERNATIONAL REALITIES 1

International Law discredited—War and law—Rights of neutrals—Neutrals and belligerents—International Law and Peace—International Law unscientific—Law of Nature—Nature of law—Purpose of law—International Law defined—Problem of law—Natural Law fallacies—Failure of International Law—"Right" of existence—Equality of States—Fundamental values—The Great War—Rights of nationalities—The great problem—Enforcement of law—Value of International Law—International Law and Diplomacy—Arbitration—International Law and Municipal Law—True sanction of International Law—The task.

CHAPTER II

NATIONALISM 23

Origin and nature of the State: Object of the State—Community of interests—Factors constituting community of interests: language; religion; political sympathies; customs, traditions; economic factor; geographical factor; external pressure—Nationalism and *Kultur*—Ethical justification of the State—The enemies of Nationalism: Statesmen; idealists—Nationalism and Internationalism—Nationalism, basis of International Law—Essentials of the State: population; territory; variety of resources; economic defense; rivers, ports; "Hinterland" doctrine; adjacent islands; conflict of interests, "free ports"; boundaries—Political essentials: "reciprocating will"; anarchism; despotism; need of guarantees by people; significance of constitutions: defects of American; defects of German Constitution; democratic government—"Moral personality" of the State: German theory of the State; Anglo-Saxon theory; merits of German theory; the individual and the State—Forces controlling destinies of nations—Ethical factor—The "conscience" of the State: *Sittlichkeit;* no common judge of nations—State a "moral person" in a legal sense—Summary.

Chapter III

The Rights of States 56

"Rights" and interests—"Declaration of Rights"; legal rights—International Law not based on abstractions—Necessity of adjusting law to reality—The "right" to exist: *status quo* not sacred; nationalism; legal right to exist—International Law universal—"Right" of Independence—Nations not truly independent; independence and recognition; status of Canada and Australia; "right" of independence an assumption; claim to freedom—"Right" of sovereignty; origin of term; sovereignty and independence; ideal of sovereignty absurd in application; theory of sovereignty of no real value—"Right" of equality: human inequalities; equality of nations; equality a logical deduction; are States truly equal?—"Right" of equality and "law of nature"; inequalities of nations; relative influence of nations; unequal representation on international courts; equality and international organization; theory of equality unsound—Summary: rights spring from recognition of interests; International Law based on realities.

Chapter IV

The Limitations of Arbitration 75

Claims of extreme Pacifists; ignorance of Arbitration—Causes of war: Spanish-American War; South African War; Russo-Japanese War; Italo-Turkish War; Balkan Wars—Treaty of Bucharest; the Great War; Arbitration not applicable; divergence of views—Scientific treatment of causes of war—Recent Arbitrations: Pious Funds Arbitration; Venezuelan Preferential Claims; Japanese house tax *et al;* Casablanca Arbitration; Savarkar Case; North Atlantic Fisheries—Dogger Bank incident—Recent diplomatic adjustments: nature of adjustments—Conclusions: I. Causes of war not trivial; II. war a last resort; III. Arbitration for unimportant matters; IV. Arbitration not justice; V. Arbitration a triumph for diplomacy; VI. Arbitration the helpmeet of diplomacy.

Chapter V

International Administration 99

World organization: Lorimer's scheme; Kant's scheme—Nations and individuals; municipal communities; international community; International Law not like municipal law—Interests of nations: international congresses; no coercion; international executive; administration of International Law; nature of; definition of rights required—International administration: Danube Commission; Suez Canal; Tangiers; Spitzbergen; Constantinople; Sanitary Board and Dette Publique; exterritorial countries; international unions, their utility; international clearing-house; Pan-American union—Summary—Conclusion.

CHAPTER VI
IGNOMINIOUS NEUTRALITY 120

Munitions embargo: United States *vs.* Great Britain; Germany *vs.* Great Britain; Germany *vs.* United States; American rights—Nature of neutrality: ships and arms; definition of munitions; enlistments; loans; rights of belligerents; Neutrality abnormal; belligerent *vs.* neutral interests; neutral rights uncertain; War of 1812; modern parallel; obligations of neutrals; difficulties of neutrality—True interests of neutrals: duty of intervention; Westlake's views; Lorimer's views; neutral cannot be indifferent—Summary.

CHAPTER VII
THE DANGERS OF PACIFISM 140

Pacifist propaganda: meaning of Militarism; meaning of Pacifism; demands on International Law; ignorance of Arbitration; Diplomacy and Arbitration; Arbitration propaganda and Europe; European problems; America not mediator of Europe—Real task: international legislation; problems of Western Hemisphere—Dangers of Pacifism: fosters cowardice and materialism; ignores spiritual values; Pacifism *vs.* Nationalism; Nationalism misunderstood; need of Nationalism; Pacifism a cause of war; Pacifism *vs.* Preparedness—Conclusion.

CHAPTER VIII
PAN-AMERICANISM 158

Misdirected idealism—The American problem: failure of United States Pan-American policy; need of law between Republics; the Monroe Doctrine interpreted by Mr. Root; Monroe Doctrine a sanction of International Law—The Monroe Doctrine a Pan-American doctrine—The creation of law: International Private Law; "conflicts of laws" within United States; Commission of Jurists; High Commission on Uniformity of Laws; the Pan-American Union; its possibilities—Duty of United States for peace.

Chapter IX

Democracy and Diplomacy 174

Causes of the Great War—The "democratization of foreign policies": popular confusion of Diplomacy with policies; statesmen determine policies—Functions of Diplomacy: success of American Diplomats; is Democracy competent to control foreign affairs? De Tocqueville's views; need of secrecy in Diplomacy; value of publicity; comprehensive knowledge required; attitude of American Democracy; Washington's policy toward France; Lincoln and *The Trent;* President Wilson and German conspiracies—Democracy and Diplomacy: issue between "Direct Government" and "Representative Government"; Democracy unable to determine policies; confidence of Democracy in its representatives—The Diplomatic Service: no parallel with Army and Navy—Objections to permanent service: "dead timber"; representative diplomats; freedom of President in his choice; permanent service undesirable; rich men not needed as diplomats; secretaries of Embassies and Legations; merit should be recognized; "Spoils System"—Summary.

Chapter X

The Substitution of Law for War . . 201

The horror of war: duelling and Arbitration; self-redress; what is peace? the horrors of peace—The European catastrophe: capable of explanation; Balance of Power; futility of Balance of Power; rights of nationalities—Sound principles: I. Community of interests: plebiscites; conflicts of interests—II. Principle of Autonomy—III. Freedom of Trade: economic interdependence; "commercial access"; wide application of principle; three principles complementary—Terms of peace—Rights and obligations: divergent views of nations; need of mutual understanding—Status of International Law: rights of foreign creditors; international torts; Conflict of Laws; International Law and war—Creation of International Law: conferences; international progress—The task.

Index 227

INTERNATIONAL REALITIES

CHAPTER I

INTERNATIONAL REALITIES

International Law has often been attacked. It has been scoffed at as being in no sense law at all. Its prestige of late, it must be admitted, has suffered considerably. It has been severely discredited—justly in some respects, most undiscriminatingly in others. Much of the criticism reveals a superficial appreciation of the facts. The most lamentable aspect of the situation, one that of necessity is not readily perceived, is that International Law has probably suffered more at the hands of its friends than of its enemies.

International Law discredited

The purpose of this chapter is, therefore, to consider frankly the various ways in which International Law has been discredited, whether justly or unjustly, and to endeavor to deal candidly with the brute facts.

First of all, it must be recognized that International Law has been seriously discredited in the eyes of many by the manner in which the Great War has been waged. It is held that the flagrant violations of accepted rules of law governing the conduct of war, by certain of the belligerents, show that International Law is entitled to little or no respect; it is impotent, a feeble reed, a "mere scrap of paper."

According to such critics, a law which cannot respond to the strain when it is most needed is a mockery, an object of derision. Such criticism, however, in spite of its apparent justification, reveals a distorted sense of proportion, a false standard of values. It proceeds from an erroneous impression, which—it must be frankly admitted—has been fostered unconsciously by many publicists, to the effect that International Law was mainly, if not primarily, concerned with the regulation of war: that in fact it had little significance except in time of war.

Curiously enough, the two Hague Peace Conferences of 1899 and 1907, which were convened for the purpose of promoting the cause of peace, have done much to confirm this impression. It is true that heroic attempts were made at these Conferences to provide adequate facilities through mediation, "Commissions of Inquiry," and particularly by Arbitration, to settle international disputes without recourse to war. But it is also true that these Conferences concentrated their labors on the making of

INTERNATIONAL REALITIES

laws to regulate the conduct of war—that abnormal state of affairs which is in fact the very negation of law.

This is not to ignore one other solitary Hague Convention concerning the Recovery of Contract Debts. Designed to eliminate one of the many causes of war, it really consecrated the most vicious principle that a nation is justified under certain questionable circumstances in resorting to force to secure payment for debts frequently of doubtful origin.

The idea that International Law should regulate war is essentially paradoxical and unsound. It is to attempt to revive the Age of Chivalry; to make wars courteous and decent; an opportunity for the display of knightly virtues. To plead for a humane war sounds almost preposterous. {War and law}

As long as wars may seem necessary and inevitable, we must, of course, insist that they be waged with due respect to the rights of humanity. It still remains true, however, that whether or no the belligerents will observe among themselves the rules of war, the dictates of humanity, there is in reality no legal method on the battle-field to compel them to do otherwise than as their own conscience and the all-con-

4 INTERNATIONAL REALITIES

trolling exigencies of military necessity may command.

<small>Rights of neutrals</small>

But you will say that the law of nations should at least uphold the rights and obligations of neutrals; that it cannot plead irresponsibility in this respect. This is undoubtedly true in large measure; but even here we must be sure of the exact conditions to which International Law should apply. If we assume, as some superficial thinkers do, that a great war is very much like a street brawl which ought not to involve any one other than the hot-headed combatants, then neutral nations are correct in insisting indignantly that the right to continue their peaceful pursuits unmolested should be scrupulously respected by the nations at war.

If, however, we are prepared to recognize the actual facts of international existence; if we realize that the nations of the earth have become so intimately interdependent that any great calamity affecting one or several of them must necessarily affect the rest, both directly and indirectly, then neutral nations cannot rightly claim their interests should not suffer material damage.

As a matter of fact, neutral nations have always recognized that war must directly affect their interests as well as the interests of the belligerents. This is evidenced by the willingness of neutrals to permit the visit, search, and even capture of their private ships on the high seas; to allow the capture of goods of a contraband character having a hostile destination; to respect formally declared, and effectively maintained, blockades; and to perform some of the irksome obligations imposed on neutrals to avoid participation in the contest.

But we must go even further. Not only must neutral nations suffer inevitably through grievous injury to their interests at the hands of belligerents; they must also recognize that the fact of the intimate interdependence of nations cannot leave neutrals entirely indifferent concerning the issues and the results of a great war. "There comes a moment," as some statesman has wisely said, "when a neutral nation is compelled to recognize that its best interests demand the triumph of one of the two sides at war." When this truth is borne in on the consciousness of a neutral nation, it must without sentiment or passion adjust its attitude accordingly. Either it must be willing to tolerate considerable interference with its technical rights by the belligerents whose side it desires

Neutrals and belligerents

to triumph, or it must openly ally itself in certain eventualities with that side, and fight as well as pray for its success. Otherwise a neutral nation may easily find itself the victim of an extraordinary situation where, in the assertion of its alleged rights, it is impelled to antagonize and harm the very belligerents whose cause it at heart most favors.

International Law and peace

The most serious indictment against International Law at the present time consists not in the manner in which this war is being waged, but in the brutal fact of war itself. The true function of International Law is not to govern war; it is to avert war. This is the real vital problem which should claim the serious attention of all thoughtful men; how can the law of nations best fulfil its functions in time of peace?

Why is it that International Law, since Grotius in 1625 tried to bring nations to their senses, has not yet found the way of avoiding war? Can it plead the impossibility of changing the evil hearts, the predatory instincts, the blind passions of men? Or must it humbly admit that it has been in error; that its alleged principles, its bold postulates, have been unsound, fallacious, and unrelated to the facts of international existence?

INTERNATIONAL REALITIES

The charge against the defective nature of man is, of course, in large measure well founded; but nothing can excuse International Law if it should be proved that its methods and its theories have been faulty and unscientific. This, I fear, ought candidly to be admitted. It would seem true that the law of nations, receiving its inception at the hands of Grotius, as it did, as a moral protest against the existing state of international anarchy, has ever since sought to play the rôle of the preacher, the teacher, the reformer, the moral idealist, rather than to serve as the jurist-consult, the lawgiver, the practical statesman.

International Law unscientific

The special evidence of this regrettable fact is to be found in the attempt to identify International Law with the Law of Nature, that mysterious, sovereign legislation, that supreme authority to which men are supposed to submit all their human affairs. The pity of it all is that the followers of Grotius would seem, in the main, to have misunderstood his purpose in invoking the Law of Nature. Grotius himself was most scientific in method, and a careful study of his statements does not indicate that he confused International Law with the Law of Nature. On the contrary, wherever he could

Law of Nature

ascertain an undoubted principle of law through an exhaustive examination of international usages, customs, and precedents of all kinds, there he was contented to rest his case. But where, as for example, in the matter of mitigating the horrors of war, he found little or no support for his humane contentions in usage, custom, or precedent, he then appealed to the Law of Nature in the obvious hope that, in the absence of a supreme Imperial or Church authority, mankind would acknowledge the dictates of reason and humanity expressed in terms of Natural Law. The most that Grotius would seem to have implied by such an appeal was a challenge to the reason of man, to his sense of equity, to his sentiments of justice. And this, apparently, is about all that any of us really mean when, outside of the field of religion, we venture to appeal to "natural rights." We merely ask each other to give the assent of our reason that certain propositions are self-evident.

There are, of course, many facts of this character which are daily accepted without question or serious discussion. We do not, however, appeal to a Law of Nature for their recognition. We know that human affairs must necessarily be carried on by discussion and argument, by an ultimate appeal to reason. If the minds of men are not convinced of the truth of an assertion, an alleged principle or right, it is useless to invoke the authority of any law, whether it be termed natural or divine.

An International Law publicist of note, in defending the Law of Nature, protested that "while you may drive it out of the front door, it will manage to gain fresh entrance through the back door or the windows." It is precisely against this kind of unguarded, careless, unscholarly mode of thought that we all should be vigilant. If by reason of conventional phraseology we are compelled to speak of Natural Law and Natural Rights, let us be clear in our own minds that we simply mean an appeal to the highest sense of justice of which reason is capable. And even then, let us be on our guard lest we fall back on a Law of Nature in order to support propositions which we may not have been able to justify by reasoned argument.

It would seem logically necessary, in avoiding recourse to an assumed Law of Nature, that we should endeavor to define more clearly what

Nature of law

we understand to be the *nature of law*. The failure to define carefully the purpose and function of law may be responsible for some of the confusion of thought that seems to exist in respect to the law of nations.

In the physical world we note the existence of certain so-called laws in accordance with which definite phenomena take place: for example, the fall of an apple in obedience to the law of gravitation. It is evident, however, that human laws are of a different character. Men are governed in other ways than as inert atoms controlled by irresistible laws; they themselves determine the laws which shall control their mutual relations. If these relations are not adjusted in an orderly fashion by common agreement, there is no possibility of an efficient social or political organization. It is of mutual concern that the interests of each and all should be duly recognized and respected.

Purpose of law

The purpose of law, expressed in its simplest terms, thus becomes evident as the protection of interests, or, as Gareis well states:

Law is the means of the peaceable regulation of the external relations of persons and their social communities among themselves.

... It does not concern itself with internal activities which belong to the domain of morals and religion. ... The nature of a legal right is such that it is always a definite interest, actually entertained by a person or a community. For the protection and guarantee of these interests, legal order expresses its commands and prohibitions, and through this guaranty interests become legal interests (legal rights).[1]

If we accept this definition of law as being scientifically exact and affording a satisfactory basis for discussion, International Law may therefore properly be defined in the words of Gareis as: "The totality of legal rules by which the public interests of States—among themselves —the international relations of States—are legally governed; and accordingly by which the common interests of States are legally protected."[2]

International Law defined

It is evident, in the light of this definition of law in general and of International Law in particular, that the practical problem is first to ascertain with precision the exact interests to be protected, and then to endeavor to discover just what law has been mutually accepted among nations to protect these interests.

Problem of law

It is here that theories of Natural Law have wrought their greatest havoc. Most of the

Natural Law fallacies

---

[1] *Science of Law*, p. 29. [2] *Ibid.*, p. 287.

writers on International Law, following in each other's footsteps, venture to lay down, with varying degrees of boldness or timidity, certain fundamental postulates, to proclaim certain "absolute," "inherent" rights of States. They assert as the keystone to the structure of International Law, the right of a State to exist. They then deduce the sovereignty of the State as a necessary attribute, though it is never very clear just what "sovereignty" really denotes. They assert the right of a State to independence, and, necessarily, to complete equality.

We have had only recently a rhetorical reaffirmation of these fundamental postulates in the form of a Declaration of Rights by the American Institute of International Law, composed of representatives of International Law societies in all of the States belonging to the Pan-American Union. Such declarations, which familiarly recall Rousseau and revolutionist literature, may pretend to define the interests of States which it is the object of International Law to protect. They do not indicate, however, from whence flow these "absolute," inherent" rights except—by a treacherous analogy to individual rights—from that mysterious authority, the Law of Nature.

As a matter of fact, if we test these theories in the laboratory of international realities, we discover that we do not always get a satisfactory reaction. We find that it is most doubtful in certain instances, such as Morocco and Persia, for example, whether a nation has a right to exist. We find that some nations are obviously not truly sovereign, completely independent, or absolutely equal by the nature of things. And yet, in the practical relations of States, it is evident that such States, whether Panama, Cuba, Belgium, or Switzerland, are to be considered as international entities with definite interests which must be properly protected.

The concepts of sovereignty, independence, and equality may serve possibly as ideals, as a goal of ambition; but from the scientific point of view they serve no practical purpose. They tend, on the contrary, to confuse, to hinder, the work of the construction of law. This is the painful confession that candor compels us to make: International Law has not yet proclaimed the Magna Carta which shall effectively regulate and protect the relations and rights of nations.

Failure of International Law

Right of existence

Nowhere is this unpleasant truth more evident than in respect to the question of the right of a State to exist. If we dispassionately review European history since the Congress of Vienna; if we consider the artificial, arbitrary manner in which boundaries have been created, peoples transferred like cattle from one State to another; if we visualize the hopeless state of anarchy that formerly existed in Morocco and now exists in Persia; if we contemplate all these facts, surely we can reach no other conclusion than that there is no absolute right of a State to exist. Boundaries that have been made arbitrarily, may as arbitrarily be remade. States now existing may be broken up or re-created along different lines. Curiously enough, portions of Empire like Canada, for example, may assume a quasi-international status without ceasing to be part of the Empire itself.

The significance of this fact concerning the right of a State to exist should be evident in relation to the development of a real science of International Law. If we have not yet defined with any accuracy the very factors, the basic elements, with which International Law must deal, it is preposterous to expect that it should be called on to protect interests which are necessarily artificial, ephemeral, and of a conflicting character.

Equality of States

If nations are not equal in moral, intellectual, or even material influence; if they have not an equal concern in the adjustment of international interests; if they have not an equal voice in the creation, the interpretation, and the enforcement of law; if, in fact, the claim to equality stands squarely in the way of world organization itself; then it is folly to insist on the concept of equality as a basic principle of the law of nations.

Fundamental values

We must therefore be sure of the exact nature of our materials in the science of International Law before we try to determine the legal rights and obligations of States. To do otherwise is to construct a bridge of wood on the assumption that we are using iron: to erect a building of chalk under the supposition that it is stone. A law of nations of such a character is of no value as a Magna Carta of international rights; it is essentially unscientific, a *modus vivendi*, a mere temporary makeshift unworthy of respect.

The Great War

The practical application of all this is obviously to be found in the Great European War.

However we may apportion the immediate responsibility for this catastrophe, we are slowly beginning to realize that its origins and its ultimate effects directly and vitally concern this question of the right of a State to exist.

Rights of nationalities

This, then, is the fundamental reality, the basic element with which International Law must deal: if we cannot concede the absolute right of a State to exist, we must recognize the rights of nationalities to exist. We must recognize the vital fact that men are bound to group together into nationalities to achieve their common ends. Until we freely concede this fact; until we try honestly and dispassionately to determine the relative rights of nationalities, potential as well as already existing; to draw boundaries with due regard for their conflicting interests and sensibilities, we have not created those reasonably permanent nations whose interests it is the function of International Law to protect.

The great problem

This, then, should be the all-absorbing preoccupation of European statesmen and the citizens of the whole world as well: to endeavor to prepare the way for a peace which shall readjust the interests of all nations on a just and

INTERNATIONAL REALITIES

firm basis. If revenge, if the desire for reparation, for power and material aggrandizement, are to be the controlling motives in the peace conference which must end this and any war; if a just, scientific appreciation of the factors which compose the fabric of international polity does not dominate its councils, we may well despair of the future of the science of International Law as well as of the peace of the world.

But, you will very properly observe, "granted that nations may yet learn to recognize and respect their mutual interests, how are these interests to be protected if there is no effective sanction for International Law?" "What kind of law is it that depends only on public opinion for enforcement, that still leaves to each nation the right of self-redress?" Such a person will be inclined to join the ranks of those who believe that a superior sanction is the chief requisite in law, and indignantly to protest that International Law is in no way entitled to be characterized as law. He will prefer to term it international morality of a feeble sort, particularly if he has received his impressions from the school of Natural Law and certain professional pacifists who are accepted as exponents of International Law.

Enforcement of law

Now it cannot be denied that the law of nations labors under this disadvantage: its edicts are occasionally treated with contempt; an international legislature, judiciary, and executive are apparently required to give it full value and power. Not only is this true, it is also evident that nations still lack that common conception of rights and obligations which is essential to enable men to unite under a common executive, legislature, and judiciary. Japan and Italy, Russia and the United States, Germany and Belgium, Haiti and Great Britain, all hold varying views of the object and powers of the State, of the rights and duties of States, of the great basic principles of justice. Until they can begin to think alike in matters of fundamental significance, it is idle to strive to force them together within a common international organization.

Value of International Law

But to admit all this is not to reduce the law of nations to a trivial and ignominious rôle. Having conceded its defects, we must likewise recognize its virtues. At a time of abnormal stress, when it is subjected to much criticism of an undiscriminating character, we must in all fairness try to appreciate the positive, ef-

INTERNATIONAL REALITIES

fective value and influence of International Law.

In ordinary times of peace the statesmen responsible for the conduct of international relations carry on an immense variety of delicate negotiations based on an avowed respect for generally accepted principles of International Law. We do not ordinarily note the successes of Diplomacy; we note only its failures. Nevertheless it is unquestionably true that in normal times of peaceful intercourse Diplomacy relies implicitly on the law of nations in the settlement of many questions, frequently of a grave character.

International Law and Diplomacy

When questions of a complicated, trying nature do not yield readily to diplomatic treatment, Diplomacy then calls in the aid of Arbitration. In this event Arbitration, though hardly functioning in every respect as a court of justice, endeavors within the scope of its powers to pay homage to the law of nations. The decisions of The Hague Arbitration Tribunals bear eloquent testimony to this fact.

Arbitration

But perhaps the most significant fact—and one that is generally ignored, even by eminent authorities of the standing of Elihu Root—is that the courts of all nations both in times of

International Law and Municipal Law

war and peace are constantly rendering important decisions based directly on the law of nations, decisions which, it must be emphasized, are duly enforced. What is more, these courts do not hesitate to declare that they are applying a law which is every whit as much entitled to respect as Municipal Law. When the Supreme Court of the United States affirms that International Law is law, it would seem, in spite of casuistic reasoning to the effect that it becomes Law only as a part of Municipal Law, there should be no further doubt concerning its complete validity. Incidentally, a most interesting instance of the homage paid to International Law in time of war is a recent decision of the Supreme Court of the German Empire upholding the right of a French citizen, now in the French army, to a patent which a German firm had sought to infringe.

True sanction of International Law

It is important that we should not fail to understand the basic principle that constrains the courts of all nations to respect the rules of International Law. The basic principle which establishes judicial precedents and crystallizes International Law as a science, is that the interests of nations must be mutually respected because of what Gareis well terms "anticipated advantages of reciprocity as well as fear of retaliation."[1]

This powerful sanction, this compulsive force of reciprocal advantage and fear of retaliation, is nothing else in its essence than the Golden Rule as formulated by Thomasius: "Do unto others for thine own sake what thou wouldst that others should do unto thee, and, in so doing, accept a law from which thou canst not escape."[2] Is it not in reality the only safe fundamental principle for international relations? As a sheer utilitarian rule of conduct—modified, if you will, by elevated ethical or religious concepts—I venture to assert that it is the most rational, practical basis for the science of International Law. There can be no more effective sanction for law than an appeal to the enlightened self-interest of men.

Our task, therefore, as defenders and upbuilders of International Law, becomes one of determining the specific mutual interests which nations are prepared to recognize; and then to endeavor, in a spirit of toleration, friendly concern, scientific open-mindedness, to formulate the legal rights and obligations which these in-

The task

[1] *Science of Law*, p. 288.
[2] Lorimer, *Institutes of Law of Nations*, I, 111.

terests entail. Having come to a substantial agreement concerning the law itself, we may then properly turn to the task of securing the most effective agencies for its interpretation and enforcement.

The nations of the earth are far from ready to be ruled by a common, sovereign, political authority. Their interests and ways of thinking are still too antagonistic for that. The great preliminary work of facilitating closer relations, of removing misunderstandings, of reconciling conflicting points of view, of identifying various interests, of fostering common conceptions of rights and obligations, remains yet to be done. We can hardly venture to express the hope that this frightful clash of interests now going on in Europe may serve in the end as a solemn and stern appeal to reason itself; that the warring nations may be preparing to meet each other in a sober, rational spirit, to seek to determine and respect their mutual interests on the practical, utilitarian basis of the Golden Rule. But surely, if such a spirit should prevail, there would be no great need of international tribunals or of "leagues to enforce peace." The absence of that spirit could only mean the necessity of future wars.

CHAPTER II

NATIONALISM

The origin and nature of the State has been a favorite theme of speculation by political theorists. We are familiar with the attempts of Hobbes and Locke to find the origin of the State in the need felt by man to escape from the chaos of an assumed state of nature. We likewise recall the theories of Rousseau and others concerning a "Social Compact."

Of much greater value than the speculations of theorists and philosophers would be a careful analysis of the reasons which led the Pilgrims to erect a State in the New World. We might better understand the origin and nature of the State if we understood the aspirations of the Poles, the ambitions of the Balkan States, and the aims of the Albanians, the latest claimants to international recognition.

The object of the State may be variously expressed as the pursuit of happiness, liberty of conscience, the good of the greatest number, power, or freedom in general. Cicero's definition of a State as "a body of men united together for the purpose of promoting their mutual safety and advantage by their combined strength"[1] is as satisfactory as any.

Community of interests

As a matter of fact, International Law is not greatly concerned with the origin and nature of the State, provided it does not exist for the purpose of annoying or plundering its neighbors. The vitally significant fact which International Law must recognize is that there is a natural tendency among men to gravitate together in distinct national groups, in accordance with common sympathies and a community of interests.

Factors constituting community of interests

It is therefore of fundamental importance to analyze carefully the factors which serve to constitute that community of interests which we must recognize as determining the separate existence of States. What are these preferences, these prejudices, these special interests which lead men to establish, maintain, and deeply cherish distinct national communities?

Language

Language would seem to be the strongest tie that binds men together. The immediate need is to readily understand each other. The sound

[1] *De Rep.* I, l. 25.

of the mother tongue creates a sense of near kinship. Confidence and sympathy are at once established. And in more highly civilized States the possession of a common literature greatly contributes to the creation of sentimental attachment and national devotion.

Religion has been a most potent factor in the creation of a community of interest, as seen in the founding of Plymouth. It is apparent in civilized, as well as primitive communities, that men prefer to associate with those who share their religious beliefs or superstitions, and worship in the same manner. The most striking example of this is found in the Ottoman Empire where the Moslems identify the State with the Church. On the other hand, the disruptive influence of rival religious cults within the State is painfully seen in Ireland where Catholics and Protestants, in the classic words of Charles Lever, "are fighting like devils for conciliation, and hating each other for the love of God." *Religion*

Common political instincts and principles naturally draw men together. Some prefer the patriarchal system of government; others the town meeting. Under their own peculiar *Political sympathies* political institutions men are thus enabled to work out their common problems with the least friction and the greatest efficiency. Even within the borders of the United States, with its bewildering confusion of racial admixtures from all over the world, it is essentially the genius of Anglo-Saxon political institutions that leavens the whole mass and enables us to organize and carry on successfully our communal life. It is this very Anglo-Saxon conception of individual liberty and political organization which, in many instances, has made America the "Land of Promise" for peoples of other nations possessing different political institutions. The United States can never be a completely unified nation unless native and naturalized Americans alike acknowledge and cherish our Anglo-Saxon institutions.

Customs, traditions

Out of these three elements—language, religion, and political instincts—spring up cherished customs, folk-lore, folk-songs, dances, social games, pride of ancestors, worship of heroes, in sum, those traditions which Lord Bryce has said constitute the greatness of nations. All these elements and traditions combine to foster that strong sentimental attachment which we characterize as patriotism, love of country. Where these elements are lacking; where a people have no vivid sense of a rich inheritance of common traditions—as in certain Spanish-American Republics—the inspiration and strength of patriotism, of devotion to country, is sadly lacking also.

The economic factor is obviously of great importance in the creation of a community of interests. This is particularly true of countries so well unified economically as Denmark, Holland, or Norway. But it is also true of countries possessing such heterogeneous elements as Austria-Hungary, for example, where there is an economic need of markets for the exchange of varied products, agricultural products for manufactured products, etc. It would seem clear that a nation which can provide a large variety of economic resources is better off than the nation which is dependent, wholly or in part, on other countries for certain necessaries. *Economic factor*

But there is another sense in which the economic factor is involved in determining a community of interests. It is the necessity of providing sufficient revenues to enable a State to carry on its political organization and effectively care for the needs of all its members. Even *Revenues* though national differences might become minimized in the process of time, there still would remain this fundamental need of an economic organization of the State. It would seem as if many Socialists in their support of Internationalism and their demand for the elimination of national boundaries quite ignored this important fact, which is indeed closely related to the great problem of a socially organized State.

<small>Geographical factor</small>

Geographical location frequently has much to do with the formation of States. Men living together on an island, for example, have every reason for uniting in a common political organization. It would have been practically impossible for England, Scotland, and Wales to maintain distinct national States. Moreover, the peculiar location of Ireland, as territory geographically appurtenant to Great Britain, demands a subordination of nationalistic desires to the common welfare of the people of the British Isles. Finland is another case in point, as also Sicily in its relation to Italy. Geographically speaking, the Bosphorus and the Dardanelles are so essential to Russia as great natural gates, that Constantinople and its environs should logically be closely related to the Empire of the Czar. Panama has a unique situation as an international highway, of greater significance to the United States and the world in general than to Colombia and the neighboring Republics.

In some instances the existence of a common enemy has served like the external pressure of hoops on a barrel to foster a national community of interests. Switzerland and Austria-Hungary are interesting examples of this. In spite of their wide diversity of interests, and even of their antagonisms, the battles of the Swiss and their constant fear of a common enemy have undoubtedly welded them into one solid nation. In the case of Austria-Hungary, the absence of a common enemy, unless the community of economic interests should prove overwhelming, would probably lead to a separation of elements so diverse and antagonistic. *External pressure*

In our analysis of the factors which help create a distinct community of interests and thus justify the establishment and maintenance of separate nations, it is evident, as in the case of Switzerland, that all these factors do not simultaneously appear in every instance. There may be an apparent clashing of interests with *Factors vary* only one special interest predominant; and yet there will be found a real community of national sympathies and interests. It is, of course, impossible to analyze as exactly as in a chemical laboratory the essential ingredients of a nation. All that we can say with confidence is, that men are drawn together in separate groups by recognized common interests, and that International Law is bound to be formed and applied in harmony with these nationalistic interests.

Nationalism and "Kultur"

Professor Vinogradoff has spoken of a nation as "a body of convictions which are more or less expressed in its manners, its language, the notions of its mind, and of its heart, the relations of its society, in fact, its whole life."[1] This would seem substantially to express all that is legitimately implied in the German use of the term *Kultur;* namely, that peculiar body of national interests which differentiate one nation from another, and which justify their separate existence.

Ethical justification of the State

This brings us to a realization of the ethical justification of the State, and of the spirit of nationalism. Is it not in reality the claim of

[1] *Hibbert Journal*, January, 1915.

freedom, the greatest possible freedom, of distinct groups of men to work out their ethical problems according to their own powers of reason and their own lights? Is it not, on a magnificent scale, the claim of the individual for freedom of thought, of investigation, of conscience, of worship itself? Is not the world vastly richer in an ethical sense through the contributions of England, Russia, Germany, the United States, Holland, and Japan?

It would seem evident that it would be a great loss to civilization if there were any serious attempt to suppress and obliterate national lines. The privilege mutually conceded by the Russians, the Spaniards, the Swedes, the Greeks, the French, and all other nationalities, to work out their own ethical problems along independent lines, would seem to be a logical necessity from the very nature of society. Not only is this true, but it would also appear, as Lorimer suggests, that "ethnology will probably teach us that the ethical ideal may be realized in accordance with ethnical ideals more diverse than we at present imagine."[1] The world may need more nationalities, rather than less!

Ethnic and ethical ideals

[1] *Institutes of the Law of Nations*, I, p. 99.

32 INTERNATIONAL REALITIES

The enemies of nationalism Statesmen

It is a painful fact that many idealists are now affiliating themselves with statesmen as the enemies of nationalism. For centuries the statesmen of Europe in deference to the vicious and disastrous principle of "Balance of Power" have oppressed and repressed nationalities; have slashed the map of Europe with a ruthless hand. Peoples have been bartered and transferred like cattle. Each attempt at an "equilibrium of forces," as for example the Treaty of Berlin, has resulted in discontent, unrest, and eventually in war. Witness the Balkan War of 1912 and its horrible aftermath, the Great War of 1914! A civilization which could tolerate the denial of the just claims of the Serbian nation, and of the Serbs as a race, has surely merited the fearful chastisement it is now receiving.

Idealists

At a time when men of affairs are just beginning to realize the utter folly of the principle of "Balance of Power," and the criminal injustice of thwarting nationalistic aspirations, it is profoundly discouraging to find idealists, in the name of world peace, the brotherhood of man, denouncing the spirit of nationalism as essentially primitive, savage, provincial, chauvinistic, narrow, antagonistic, and inimical to the spirit of Internationalism. Some go so far, even, as to quote with evident approval the cynical sneer of Johnson that "patriotism is the last refuge of scoundrels."

It is difficult to understand how love of family, devotion to one's nearest of kin, interest in the concerns of his neighbor, loyal service to his own immediate community, consecration to the welfare of the greatest number, deep, fervent love of country—in sum, how such patriotism is in any way ignoble, or hostile to the great cause of Internationalism. It is difficult, in fact, to understand how any man can love and serve mankind in general if he has not first learned to love and serve his own family and community. The world may well be impatient of the vague preachings of idealists which do not find their logical expression in local service. There is surely no reason to doubt that the spirit of enlightened self-interest should inevitably lead a man from selfish concerns to altruistic concern in the affairs of his neighbor, and so by natural steps to a comprehension of the rights and needs of mankind in general, and of nations in particular.

Nationalism and Internationalism

Nationalism, basis of International Law

Whatever the crimes of statesmen and the follies of idealists, we are now confronted with the spirit of nationalism in all its dynamic, explosive power, its crude reality, and naked truth. There is a Russian proverb to the effect that if one buries the Slavic spirit beneath the strongest fortress, it will inevitably blow the fortress to pieces. It is this power, whether it be in Germany, Russia, Serbia, or France, that is now shaking and staggering the world. Whether we like it or not, this is the brute fact we must face. Shall we continue to try to suppress, restrict, or thwart the legitimate claims of nationalism? Will we not rather frankly recognize this inherent tendency of men to group together according to their mutual preferences, their national community of interests? Is it not the duty of thoughtful men to grapple honestly with this basic problem, and endeavor in a scientific spirit to discover the laws of association which should determine the formation and development of nations? It would seem as if the Great War were a demonstration of the failure of unscientific principles among nations, and of the supreme need of other principles. International Law can no longer rest on a fictitious *status quo*. It cannot

NATIONALISM

be asked to protect interests which are false or criminal.

Essentials of the State

If we concede, therefore, the inevitability, and the justice of nationalism, as the only sound basis of the whole system of International Law, we are led to inquire: what are the true essentials of the State as an international entity? What are the laws of association which determine the organization and development of nations? What do men require in order to work out their national problems?

Population

The first essential would obviously appear to be an adequate number of men vividly conscious of their mutual interests, able to maintain a State worthy of international respect, and to fulfil its international obligations. It is difficult to treat seriously so minute a Republic as that of San Marino, or Andorra. A certain weight of numbers is required in a State to warrant its formal inclusion in the family of nations. Small aggregations of men feeling a strong community of interests more naturally find their interests best served as autonomous communities under the protection and guidance of larger States. If, however, it should become apparent that the Jews were fully prepared in sufficient numbers to maintain a separate national State, it would seem that somewhere on the face of the wide world a place might be found to permit them, in all justice, to achieve their nationalistic aspirations.

Territory

Territory would obviously seem to be the next essential of the State. It is, of course, possible, theoretically, in an advanced stage of society, to postulate a political association of men such as the Jews or the Gypsies having no territorial possessions whatever, very much as it is possible that Switzerland might maintain a navy without seaports of its own. Under actual conditions, however, it is evident that nations need definite lands to cultivate, and settle on, for the effective protection and advancement of their interests.

Variety of resources

The chief characteristic of national territory, then, is a sufficient area with a variety of resources adequate for the support of its inhabitants. Under modern standards of living and intimate intercommunications, it is, of course, well-nigh impossible for any nation to be completely self-sufficient. There is a vivid and, at the same time, a gratifying sense of interdependence among nations. It still remains true, however, that the ideal condition for a nation is to possess such a variety of natural resources as to preserve it from the unfortunate status of dependence on any other nation. The United States is wonderfully blessed in this regard; Montenegro and Albania are most unfortunate. In fact, when a nation like Montenegro finds itself so restricted in territory that it cannot support its people or maintain its government, it then becomes necessary to expand or expire.

This economic need of adequate territory and resources is increasingly apparent, in view of the disguised kind of warfare in the international struggle for existence and for commercial expansion, which takes the form of protective tariffs. There is something ominous in the announced intention of the Entente Allies to unite in concerted measures for the permanent protection of their industries and commerce. Under such hostile conditions in times of peace, it becomes of the most vital importance to nations that they should be as far as possible self-sufficient in respect to extent of territory and variety of resources. *Economic defense*

The adequate protection of economic interests, as also the military security of the State as a whole, demands the control of natural *Rivers, ports* avenues of communication and transportation, such as rivers, valleys, bays, coasts, and especially ports. It has been well said that "ports are the lungs by which nations breathe," and a nation shut off from the ocean highways of commerce, as Serbia has been deliberately shut off, is in grave danger of economic, as well as of military, strangulation.

The economic development and security of a nation is greatly facilitated if it completely controls a great navigable river—the Mississippi, for example. This development and security is correspondingly endangered if, as in the case of the Danube, other nations share, or even forbid, such control.

"Hinterland" doctrine

It is likewise of vital importance to a nation to possess the "hinterland" lying behind a valuable strip of coast, or forming the natural drainage area of a great river system. Vice versa, it is essential to a nation to possess the coast forming a natural outlet for the "hinterland," as in the case of Montenegro, which was arbitrarily denied possession of Cattaro, its natural port of entry. The ownership by the United States of the Alaskan Panhandle, the long narrow strip of coast barring exit and egress to the natural ports of the Canadian

NATIONALISM

Northwest, is an obstacle in the way of the proper development of that "hinterland."

This principle of the "hinterland" has been recognized by the European Powers in their scrambles for territory in Africa. There is no reason whatever why it should not be recognized in any future readjustments of territory both in Europe and America.

Of similar importance is the principle that a nation should properly own and control the islands lying off its coasts. The return of Heligoland to Germany by England was thus entirely fitting. So likewise the cession of the Bermudas and the Bahamas to the United States would be eminently just. A fair *quid pro quo* would be the Panhandle of Alaska. *[Adjacent islands]*

There are, of course, situations where there is an obvious conflict of interests, as in the case of Trieste. This port, formerly Italian and still Italian, probably, in racial sympathies, is essential to the Austrian "hinterland." In all such anomalous situations, if a territorial readjustment be found excessively difficult, the least that can be conceded is the establishment of "free ports," as in the case of Salonica, a Greek port subject to the free use of Serbia. *[Conflict of interests. Free ports]*

Boundaries

Considerations such as these must be held in mind when it comes to defining the boundaries of nations. Not only must nationalistic claims be respected as far as possible, but economic and military interests must be adequately protected. Mountains, as a rule, make better boundaries than rivers. The economic and other interests of the people inhabiting a river-valley—the Rhine, for example—are usually so identical as to render a river boundary artificial and obnoxious, a constant source of friction. Military considerations may largely determine the control of ocean straits and channels. Russia, for this reason alone, if for no other, is bound to view with apprehension the control by other nations of Constantinople and its straits which constitute the natural entrance, the *couloir* of Southern Russia. So likewise, though we speak of the "neutralization" of the Panama Canal, an artificial ocean strait, its absolute control and protection must of necessity remain with the United States.

Political essentials

Such in brief are some of the physical essentials of a State. The next essential to be considered is the political constitution of the State viewed from the international standpoint. If nations are to exist as separate entities, how are

NATIONALISM 41

they to organize most effectively to meet together, and transact their mutual affairs? How can they best guarantee respect for their mutual rights and the fulfilment of their just obligations?

Lorimer holds that the possession of what he terms a "reciprocating will" is an essential characteristic of the State. If nations are to enter into agreements to respect and guarantee each other's rights, they must have the will and the power to carry out their agreements. An anarchical State would be an obvious impossibility from the international point of view, as there could be no sure means of intercourse nor certainty of respect for international rights.

"Reciprocating will"

Anarchism

If an anarchical State is incapable of expressing and enforcing an international will, so likewise a despot is not properly qualified to pledge the will of a State. The people may be physically incapable of restraining their ruler; he may arbitrarily contract loans, hypothecate the revenues of the State for generations, and enter into momentous obligations. He may cede valuable portions of territory, or even hand over the entire State. Other nations, to

Despotism

their own advantage, may consider a despot properly qualified to perform such acts. Yet the fact remains that the "reciprocating will" of an entire people may have been completely ignored, and the right of nullifying the acts of their ruler held in abeyance until the opportunity to revolt should arise.

Need of guarantees by people

Under such conditions international agreements cannot be allowed to rest on so uncertain and untrustworthy a basis. What is demanded, in the name of international fair play and reason, would seem clearly to be the "reciprocating will" of a whole people. They must know what they are assenting to, and must not be committed without their consent to more than they are willing or able to fulfil. This necessarily implies that international treaties should never attempt to place a burden on subsequent generations; and that the terms of such agreements must needs be for brief periods of time, subject to the right of abrogation or renewal.

Significance of constitutions. Defects of American

Viewed in this light, the internal constitution of States is of great concern to nations in their mutual relations. It is curious to reflect in this connection that the United States, owing to its peculiar Constitution, is not able effectively to safeguard the rights of aliens as guaranteed by treaties and International Law. This fact has been clearly brought out in the questions concerning the rights of the Japanese in California. The inability of the United States to control the acts of the separate States of the Union is no satisfactory answer to the just complaints of foreigners and of their aggrieved governments. Legislation is urgently required to give the Federal Government the power and the authority necessary to make its "reciprocating will" toward other nations completely effective.

Consider also the case of Germany. The control of the German Empire by the Kingdom of Prussia; the control of Prussia in turn by a Junker minority; and the control of that minority by a militaristic class which may at any moment precipitate a gigantic war, is a portentous fact which has long kept the whole of Europe in a constant state of fear, and subject to the burden of impossible armaments. Whatever the rights or wrongs of the Great War may be, it would seem certain that the welfare of Europe and of the whole world demands that power of such terrible magnitude—the power

Defects of German Constitution

to pledge or overthrow the "reciprocating will" of the German Empire—should be taken from the hands of a militaristic minority, and placed in the hands of the German people as a whole.

<small>Democratic government the ideal government</small>

The ideal government, therefore, from the international point of view, is the democratic, broadly representative government, whether as a republic or a monarchy, which by constitutional provisions will make certain that the will of a whole people is properly pledged and enforced, and is in slight danger of being misrepresented or improperly controlled. As Lorimer truly says, "Publicity is of the very essence of constitutional government, whether monarchical or republican. Despotic and even oligarchic governments may tell a false story to the world; but a constitutional government thinks aloud and invites the world to listen. Hence the exceptional international confidence which constitutional States always inspire."[1]

<small>"Moral personality" of the State</small>

The interesting question naturally presents itself at this point whether the State is to be considered as a "moral personality." Is it controlled by the same standards of conduct as the individual, as asserted by Ex-President

[1] *Institutes of the Law of Nations*, I, p. 192.

Taft; or is it a distinct organism, controlled by utterly different laws, as asserted by the German school of political theorists?

Bluntschli has stated the German theory of the State in the following striking words:

German theory of the State

> An oil-painting is something other than a mere aggregation of drops of oil and color; a statue is something other than a combination of marble particles; a man is not a mere quantity of cells and blood-corpuscles; and so too the nation is not a mere sum of citizens; and the State is not a mere collection of external regulations. . . . In the State, spirit and body, will and active organs are necessarily bound together in one life. The one national spirit, which is something different from the average sum of the contemporary spirit of all citizens, is the spirit of the State; the one national will, which is different from the average will of the multitude, is the will of the State. . . . To extend the reputation and the power of the State, to further its welfare and its happiness, has universally been regarded as one of the most honorable duties of gifted men.[1]

Such a conception seems to the Anglo-Saxon mind rather as the creation of a poetic imagination than a statement of fact. In our devotion to the spirit of individualism we are accustomed to think of the State somewhat as a club, a corporation, a partnership for the transaction

Anglo-Saxon theory

[1] *Theory of the State*, 2d ed., pp. 19–22.

of business in accordance with the code of honor and the standards of conduct of the individual members of the club or corporation. It was probably for this reason that the statement of ex-President Taft to the effect that a nation should submit its questions of honor to Arbitration, as readily as an individual, was received with such general assent.

Merits of German theory

In spite of its exaggeration and unfortunate manifestations, the German point of view concerning the State is nevertheless entitled to thoughtful consideration. It will at once be conceded that the State cannot have all the attributes of the individual: it cannot marry, love, hate, suffer, sacrifice itself, sport, gamble, amuse itself, etc. Must it not be recognized that corporate responsibility is different from individual responsibility? A trustee may take chances with his own funds that he will not take with funds intrusted to him. A man will readily sacrifice himself, and at times the interests of his immediate family, to meet what he deems to be an obligation of honor. The State cannot in the same manner sacrifice itself or the interests of existing or future generations. Washington had to face such a problem when in 1793 it was made to appear that the

NATIONALISM

United States was in honor bound by its treaty of alliance with France to take up arms against England. With serenity of judgment and conscience—probably against his personal inclinations—Washington was able to withstand the sentimentalists and pledge the United States to an attitude of neutrality, a policy which has since been recognized as serving the highest interests of the nation.

There is a profound degree of truth in Bluntschli's statement that "the one national will, which is different from the average will of the multitude, is the will of the State." The average will of the multitude may often represent a compromise, not a final, incontrovertible judgment. The views of the majority may frequently be wrong, and the minority right. The exaggerated sense of obligation and honor of either the majority, the minority, or of those charged with immediate responsibility may be utterly dangerous in its counsels.

Distinction between the individual and the State

Those on whom rests the burden of directing the affairs of a nation come to realize that the destinies of nations are governed by mysterious, all-powerful forces which the intellects of statesmen can but feebly apprehend. There

Forces controlling destinies of nations

are moments when the personal predilections, the sensitive standards of honor, and the individual sense of responsibility of rulers, their advisers, or of any considerable number of conscientious men, count for very little in the face of these elemental forces, these supreme laws that seem to be controlling the destinies of nations. Whether it be the Reformation, the American Revolution, the Civil War, or the Great War of 1914, individual standards of conduct are of little service to such men as William of Orange, Washington, Lincoln, Lee, Sir Edward Grey, von Jagow, President Wilson, and all others burdened with the cares of State. They cannot turn for guidance in their bewilderment to the uninformed judgment of the people at large, nor can they even appeal with confidence to the judgment of posterity. It is no wonder that men in such great national crises seek in all humility for Divine guidance, or are tempted to become fatalists. The imponderable, unseen factors affecting the fate of individuals in the aggregate, and determining inexorably the destinies of nations, are so mysterious and powerful that the only safe rule for statesmen to try to follow is the old Roman maxim, *Salus populi suprema lex*, well interpreted by Spinoza as meaning that the supreme law of the State is "the security of the State."[1] It may be exceedingly difficult at times to see clearly where the security of the State may lie, as in the case of Bulgaria, Roumania, and Greece in the Great War. It would seem clear, however, that the security of the State is a sounder principle of action than the suggestions of sentimentalists and morbid individualists. Only an inability to make clear distinctions can lead one to assert in sweeping terms that the same laws control the State as the individual.

This is not to eliminate the ethical factor from national and international affairs. Christianity, for example, has accomplished very much in introducing more humane and just standards among nations, and must continue to exert its beneficent influence. So far as men are able to act with complete freedom of will, ethical considerations in affairs of state can never be ignored. There must be no confusion of thought, however, no false analogies concerning the individual and the State. Granted that it is not easy to differentiate clearly the nature of the State from the nature of the individual, this much would seem cer-

Ethical factor not eliminated

[1] *Theologico-Political Treatise*, chap. XIX.

tain, namely, that the same forces and principles do not operate on both alike.

The "conscience" of the State

In earlier times the British Chancellor of the Exchequer was given the quaint title of "Keeper of the King's Conscience," and as such was charged with the solemn responsibility of seeing that justice was properly administered. If we ask ourselves who is the keeper of the "conscience" of the State, who is responsible for the administration of international justice, who is in a position to pass judgment on the international acts of the State; the answer is not easy to find.

"Sittlichkeit"

It is true that some men, who have been stirred by the "vision splendid" of a great "Federation of Man," believe in the efficacy of an international "*Sittlichkeit*," a universal concept of rights and obligations, a worldwide public opinion capable of judging the acts of nations. Such idealists—and they are not all of the irresponsible variety—would gladly submit all of the international acts of the State not only to the judgment but to the final decision of other States. They would forbid aggressive action by any nation to obtain redress for, or prevent wrong-doing, cruelty, attacks on the lives and property of its citizens by other nations. All such matters as well as questions affecting the "vital interests" and the "honor" of nations should be referred without hesitancy to international inquiry or Arbitration. Arbitrators, free from all national and racial prejudices, detached from the atmosphere of world politics, and blessed with transcendent wisdom, should be allowed to judge the acts of England in Egypt, France in Morocco, Russia in Persia, and the United States in Mexico and Colombia! If these infallible jurists should decide that the sovereign rights of the Egyptians had been outraged, then England must get out of Egypt. If Colombia was entitled to do as it pleased with the Isthmus of Panama, then the United States should hand over the Panama Canal to its rightful sovereign!

Reasoning of this character is based on an extraordinary misunderstanding of the stern facts of international existence. It falsely assumes a family of nations composed of peoples possessing common standards of right and wrong, common conceptions of rights and obligations. It falsely assumes the existence of a world Areopagus capable of legislating con-

False assumptions

cerning the vital interests of States. It falsely assumes the existence of a supreme court of the world entirely competent to administer absolute justice between Briton and Persian, Russian and Chinese, German and Japanese. It falsely assumes the existence of an international executive and police, able to carry out the decrees of this Areopagus and supreme court. In sum, it is on premises of this fictitious character that the bold assertion, that there no longer exists any justification for acts of international self-redress, is based.

<small>No common judge of nations</small>

It is a simple matter for people who reason in this free manner to hold that nations are not the "keepers of their own conscience." For those, however, who recognize the hard realities of international existence, who perceive the lamentable lack of a genuine community of ideas, of principles of action, of a thorough mutual understanding among nations, and specifically, the lack of a common superior to make, administer, interpret, and enforce law, it is impossible to intrust the honor, the vital interests, the "conscience" of any State to the sense of honor and the judgment of other nations. In the broadest possible sense, then, it would seem true, as Lorimer points out, that "No free state puts either its conscience or its judgment wholly into the keeping of any other."[1]

In appropriating thus the metaphor of the "conscience of the State," we do not, of course, mean to fall into the error of attributing to the State the moral personality of the individual. We need to be on our guard against that dangerous fallacy. If we speak of the State as a "moral person," as the courts frequently do, we must be sure of our terms. We should recall that, as an international entity possessing a "reciprocating will," with which other States must deal, a nation is bound to prosecute its rights and fulfil its obligations. This is all that the courts would seem to imply, and all that International Law assumes, namely— that in its legal capacity to possess rights and incur obligations, the State, to that extent, is a "moral person." Unduly to expand the use of this term, as meaning the unrestricted application of individual standards of conduct to the acts of the State, is to lead to confusion of thought and to dangerous conclusions.

State a "moral person" in a legal sense

[1] *Institutes of the Law of Nations*, I, p. 216.

Summary

By way of summary, in our consideration of the nature of the State and of the claims of Nationalism, that dynamic force which compels recognition as the very basic factor of International Law, we have been led to the following general conclusions:

I. The inevitable tendency of men to group together into nations in accordance with definite preferences, sympathies, and a genuine community of interests must clearly be recognized. It is an elemental force which cannot be ignored or thwarted. It should be allowed to take its natural course in accordance with certain simple principles.

This community of interests necessarily varies in different nations but can usually be clearly ascertained. It may include common sympathies of language, religion, political instincts, social and other traditions. It certainly demands a community of economic interests.

II. The main essentials of a properly organized nation formed in accordance with a recognized community of interests would seem to be: (1) a population bound together with common sympathies, and adequate to render the State vigorous and self-sufficient; (2) territory including varied resources, with rivers, ports, and all natural facilities for economic organization; and (3) a government so representative of the people as to enable them to deal effectively with other nations and fulfil their just obligations.

III. The State is something different from the individuals who compose it, and is not governed by identical laws. It is a profound error to confuse individual standards with national standards of conduct. The State is not a moral personality in the same sense as a man. Owing to the imponderable, unseen factors affecting its destinies, acts of the State cannot be judged by contemporary opinion or that of posterity with absolute finality. There is as yet no universal authority to judge fairly the deeds of nations. The only safe rule, therefore, for statesmen who fully appreciate the nature of their responsibilities is the rule emphasized by Spinoza: that the supreme law of the State is the security of the State.

CHAPTER III

THE RIGHTS OF STATES

"Rights" and interests

There is a marked tendency with most men, when their interests are endangered, to protest loudly against the invasion of their "rights." If they are uncertain concerning the legal basis of their "rights," they appeal to "natural rights" and to the "rights of humanity." This is also true of nations. We have heard much of late of the "rights" of neutrals. In the case of both men and nations, what is frequently at stake is not a *right*, but an *interest*.

"Declaration of Rights"

A recent interesting example of this tendency to assert a "right" in the abstract is the action of the newly formed American Institute of International Law, composed of representatives of the nations of the Western Hemisphere, in issuing to the world a heroic "Declaration of Rights," a kind of international Magna Carta. We here find asserted in phraseology recalling the seventeenth and eighteenth century school of political theorists, the "rights" of States to existence, independence, sovereignty, and equality, in accordance with "the laws of nature and of nature's God." Mr. Root, ex-Secretary of State—a member of the institute—has felt impelled to come forward as a valiant and needed champion of this extraordinary Declaration.

It would seem as if no argument were required to demonstrate that legal rights cannot be based on abstractions, on assumptions, on "inherent," "absolute," "primordial," "fundamental" rights, to quote the terms used by many writers on International Law. Rights, as we have seen, spring from the legal recognition of definitely determined interests. Any other kind of alleged right belongs in the sphere of morals and has no place in a science of law. *Legal rights*

International Law, as I have tried to point out in the opening chapter, has been badly discredited of late; and it has been discredited quite as much by its friends as by its enemies. The attempts to base international rights on mere abstractions, on vague appeals to the Law of Nature and the rights of mankind, are bound to awaken distrust and even derision. The interests of nations, as of men, cannot be regulated by any such artificial system of law. *International Law not based on abstractions*

Necessity of adjusting law to reality

It is profoundly discouraging that the Great War, with all its appalling losses and its lessons, does not yet seem to have convinced many earnest thinkers that International Law has heretofore rested on a false basis; that the *interests* of nations have not been accurately formulated or adequately safeguarded. A calamity of this magnitude surely should compel men to abandon abstractions, and to deal with the great realities of international existence. Instead of vainly trying to adjust these realities to conform with theories of law, it is time we endeavored honestly to readjust the law to meet the actual necessities of nations. That, at least, is the task we have here set ourselves. It would therefore seem necessary to weigh and consider these "fundamental postulates" of International Law, namely, the "right" of a State to existence, independence, sovereignty, and equality.

The "right" to exist

When it is asserted that a State has the "right" to exist, it can hardly mean that all existing States have the right: Morocco, Persia, Turkey, for example. If a State deteriorates in its domestic life, and becomes incapable of maintaining a political organization, it may require something of the nature of a protectorate or an international receivership, as in the case of Persia. If it misbehaves in such a way as to become a menace to the welfare of other nations, it will deserve either restraint of its freedom or actual extinction as a separate nation. Society does not guarantee to the individual any legal or moral right to exist. It protects him from assassination but does not allow him to continue to exist if he is a menace to the community as a whole. His right is not "absolute"; it is a qualified right. And so it must be with nations; they have no "absolute right" of existence.

Nor does this "right" to exist imply the maintenance of a sacred *status quo*. Though great respect is due the established order of things to avoid uncertainty and unrest, there is no possibility of perpetuating, under the name of law, an iniquitous *status quo* created, after the manner of the Congresses of Vienna and Berlin, in flagrant disregard of the legitimate aspirations of whole nations. If justice is not done to the just demands of nationalism, revolution and war are bound to establish a new *status quo*.

"Status quo" not sacred

60 INTERNATIONAL REALITIES

Nationalism basis of "right" to exist

The right to exist, therefore, becomes primarily the recognition of the tendency of men to group together in separate national communities in accordance with their different preferences and interests. This is the solid rock of International Law. Before an interest can be protected, it must be properly defined; and there should be no protection of unjust interests. Before International Law, therefore, can effectively apply between definite international persons, it must make sure that these entities, these national interests are normal, logical, and worthy of protection. We must first determine the basic factors before we can create a system of law. We must first show the right of States to exist.

Legal right to exist

In what sense, then, may we properly speak of the legal right of a State to exist? In its essence it would seem to flow from the formal recognition which States extend to each other in one form or another. When States are confronted with the fact of the existence of another State, they have practically the choice of three alternatives. They may do as Rome often did, seek to destroy the State; they may decide on non-intercourse, a practical impossibility under modern conditions; or, realizing the inevitability of intercourse, they will extend to the new State a formal recognition. This recognition constitutes, then, a mutual guarantee between nations, great and small, of their legal right to a separate existence in order to realize their own aspirations and destinies.

This legal right, moreover, applies to all States without discrimination, once they are definitely recognized. International Law, therefore, is not restricted, as some writers would hold, to the so-called civilized States. Though European in origin, the law of nations is universal in application, and in its evolution as a science.

<small>International Law universal</small>

The "right" of independence, theoretically, is a necessary corollary of the "right" of a State to exist. It was particularly of value in the sixteenth and seventeenth centuries when the smaller nations were struggling to emerge from the control of Kings and Emperors. The separate existence of States required that there should be no intermeddling, no intervention in each other's affairs. It was logically necessary to postulate a "right" of complete independence.

<small>The "right" of independence</small>

Nations not truly independent of each other

As a matter of fact, the conception of States completely independent of each other, living, as it were, in a fictitious state of nature, is in antagonism with the conception of a community of nations accepting a common law. Once States have recognized each other's existence; have adjusted themselves to the necessity of intercourse; and have acknowledged mutual rights and obligations, they have ceased to be truly independent; they have admitted their interdependence. Take for example the question of the rights of aliens. It is evident that nations are not free independently to do as they please with the stranger who may be travelling or sojourning within their borders.

Independence and recognition

Furthermore, it is not necessary that a State should be absolutely independent to entitle it to international recognition. Cuba, for instance, though seriously restricted both in its internal and external freedom of action by its treaty engagements with the United States, is nevertheless a nation having all the essentials of an international personality. Panama, with much less freedom, owing to the paramount interests of the United States, is also a separate nation. Switzerland, though denied the right of aggressive action as a neutralized State protected by the Powers, is none the less a nation.

It is of particular interest to note that Canada and Australia, though integral parts of the British Empire, are in process of assuming an international status. Sir Wilfrid Laurier has been quoted to the effect that Canada possesses the essential characteristics of a nation. It has carried on diplomatic negotiations with the United States and Japan; and has been conceded the right to become a party to certain international agreements relating to the Postal Union and Wireless Telegraphy, etc. There is nothing inherently incompatible in admitting the possibility of such States as Canada, Australia, and South Africa becoming, like Bavaria, international States, though still retaining a dependent relation to their respective Empires.

Status of Canada and Australia

For these reasons, therefore, it is erroneous, both in theory and practice, to speak of a "right" of independence. It is without justification, and is entirely misleading. It is an abstract assumption having little relation to reality.

"Right" of independence an assumption

"Right" of independence the claim to freedom

In its simplest terms, the claim to the "right" of independence is merely the claim of a nation to a certain degree of freedom. "The international State"—to quote the words of Lorimer—"whether great or small, must thus be a *separate* State. As the claim to recognition is a logical abandonment of independence, it is a logical profession of separate political life."[1]

The "right" of sovereignty

The "right" of sovereignty, like the "right" of independence, is theoretically a logical corollary of the "right" to exist. If a State is to be allowed to enjoy and maintain its own separate existence; if, as a responsible, international personality, it is to possess a "reciprocating will," it must possess *freedom* of will; it cannot be subject to the sovereign will of another.

Origin of term

This concept also had a special significance in the sixteenth and seventeenth centuries when the smaller States were endeavoring to assert their own personalities, and were called on to acknowledge allegiance to sovereigns of both Church and State. It was desirable to stress the idea of sovereignty; to emphasize the com-

[1] *Institutes of the Law of Nations*, I, p. 140.

THE RIGHTS OF STATES

plete freedom of nations to work out their own problems as "sovereign, political units."

In this sense, then, sovereignty and independence are virtually synonymous terms, when employed by writers on International Law in respect to the external freedom of the State. "External sovereignty," in the words of Wheaton, is "the independence of one political society in respect to all other political societies."[1]

Sovereignty and independence

If we attempt to apply this idea of sovereignty to concrete instances we find not only that it does not work, but that it results in a *reductio ad absurdum*. In the case of Cuba, or of Panama, which do not possess complete freedom of action, there is evidently an *impairment* of sovereignty. It is necessary to admit the existence of a *super*-sovereign! To speak of a "Suzerainty," as in the case of Egypt, is to employ a euphonism. To speak of any of these States as "Half-Sovereign" is to render the theory of sovereignty ridiculous. To meet such dilemmas, namely, the existence of certain international personalities having a qualified status as nations, defenders of the

Idea of sovereignty absurd in application

[1] *Elements of International Law*, edited by Dana, 8th ed., p. 32.

"right" of sovereignty are driven to invoke the fiction that such States are *still sovereign* by reason of the fact that they have exercised their sovereign will in consenting to restrictions on their sovereignty! "What the King consents to, he commands."

Theory of sovereignty of no real value

It is difficult, therefore, to see any real value in a modern doctrine of sovereignty. Even if applied to the internal freedom of the State, to its "exclusive, sovereign jurisdiction" within its own borders, the theory breaks down. As we have already noted, no nation, for instance, is absolutely free to do as it pleases with the stranger within its gates. A large part of diplomatic negotiations is concerned with the protection of aliens from arbitrary and unjust claims to "exclusive, sovereign jurisdiction."

For the practical purposes of International Law, therefore, it would seem eminently desirable to discard completely the idea of the "right" of sovereignty. It is particularly desirable, if one looks forward to the time when portions of Empire, like Canada and Bavaria, having no pretensions to sovereignty, may assume a more definite international status; when the nations of the earth may be willing to merge their interests more completely, and the claims of petty "sovereign" States would stand in the way of international harmony and order.

The "right" of equality

No political dogma has had greater acceptance or been in more flagrant opposition with the facts than the assertion of the Declaration of Independence that, "All men are created equal." As an ideal, a goal of perfection, it is worthy of all respect. As a statement of fact, or as a sacred guarantee, it is of doubtful value.

Human inequalities

The more one studies actual conditions in human society, the more he is aware of the existence of distinct inequalities and serious handicaps among men from the moment of birth. He sees that even "before the law," position, wealth, intellect, and personality are all factors likely to affect the administration of justice. In fact, it would seem to be the first duty of the court to clearly admit such inequalities in order that a real equality may be restored and justice accorded. Moreover, when we speak of "the equality of men before the law," we must bear in mind the fact that, if any men as individuals or as a class are denied an equal participation in the making of the law, they cannot be said to be equals when it comes

68   *INTERNATIONAL REALITIES*

to the application of the law. All such disabilities, whether inherited, accidental, physical, intellectual, or political, testify to the fact all men are not created equal, nor can they even be guaranteed a perfect equality. It is obvious that the much-vaunted "equality of men" vanishes in the light of cold reality. It is hardly anything more than a pious moralization, an abstract assumption, a remote ideal.

Equality of nations

So it has been with the doctrine of the equality of States, which has been curiously assimilated to the doctrine of the equality of man. It has been loudly and frequently proclaimed as a self-evident truth. A familiar statement of this sort was made by Chief Justice Marshall that "No principle of general law is more universally acknowledged than the perfect equality of nations. Russia and Geneva have equal rights."[1] And now we have the brave assertion of the American Institute of International Law: "Every nation is in law and before law the equal of every other State composing the society of nations, and all States have the right to claim and, according to the Declaration of Independence of the United States, to assume, among the Powers of

[1] *The Antelope*, 10 Wheaton, 66, 122.

THE RIGHTS OF STATES

the earth, the separate and equal station to which the laws of nature and of nature's God entitle them!"

The equality of States is of course as much a logical deduction from the theory of the "right" to exist, as the "right" of independence and sovereignty. At a time when States were struggling to emerge and to assert their separate existence; when their claims and their diplomatic representatives were treated with contempt, it was expedient to insist on the equality of nations. The admission of inequality, like the admission of dependence and allegiance, was to endanger the separate, free existence of a State claiming a distinct international personality.

Equality a logical deduction

The original utility of the concept of equality is apparent. What, however, is its value and truth in relation to the facts and conditions of to-day? Are States truly equal "in law and before the law"? Have they the "right" to "claim and to assume among the Powers of the earth, the separate and equal station to which the laws of nature and of nature's God entitle them"? Have Liberia and Great Britain, Haiti and the United States an "equal station"?

Are States truly equal?

"Right" of equality and "law of nature"

As we have before had occasion to observe, it is of slight value to invoke the "Law of Nature and of Nature's God" as the basis of the legal organization of society. Appeals of this character to a vague absolute law, to Divine ordinances, are in themselves a confession of weakness of argument, an inability to appeal to man's reason, an open evasion, in fact, of the realities which lie open to every man's comprehension. Men do not accept with blind allegiance any law imposed by an absolute sovereign. They are not inert atoms; they make their own laws.

Inequalities of nations

When we come to examine dispassionately these realities, we see that nations are unequal with respect to population, natural resources, geographical location, wealth, etc., etc. As peoples, they are unequal in physical stamina, moral worth, and general efficiency. We are bound to recognize the "primacy" of certain Great Powers.

Relative influence of nations

In great international conferences, such as at The Hague or the Naval Conference of 1909 at London, it is evident that the opinions of Liberia and Great Britain cannot possibly be of equal weight when it comes to the enactment

THE RIGHTS OF STATES

of positive legislation. In fact, the Naval Conference, consisting as it did only of representatives of the Great Powers, was an open denial of the claim of equality.

Not only are the Great Powers unable to admit a "perfect equality of nations" in the making of International Law; they are unable to admit an equality of representation on the International Prize Court—already agreed on but never established—or on any proposed Court of Arbitral Justice. *Unequal representation on international courts*

Nations such as Great Britain, Germany, and the United States, cannot safely intrust their vast interests to the decisions of judicial representatives of the great majority of smaller States, or to the free vote and disposition of an unrestricted democracy of nations. The pretensions to a perfect equality constitute, in fact, the greatest obstacle in the way of any kind of international organization, even of the limited character of the Conferences at The Hague. If it should be found possible to organize the community of nations so as to insure greater security and justice for the weak as well as the strong nations, then the smaller States, in return for such great benefits, would *Equality and international organization* do well to abandon their pretensions to equality. The frank admission of the palpable fact of their inequalities would do much to facilitate the task of international polity.

Theory of equality unsound

From every point of view, therefore, whether of theory, of practice, or of hopes for the future, the theory of the equality of States is unsound. Except as the claim to what Bonfils has well termed "respect for political personality"—a sort of plea for international good manners—it is of doubtful value. The law of nations demands something more solid as a foundation.

Summary

By way of summary, then, these "inherent," "absolute," "fundamental rights" of States would seem, in last analysis, to be reduced to the following "inherent" values.

Right to exist

The right to exist springs from the mutual recognition which States accord to each other as a guarantee of their separate freedom. This right is not absolute: it is qualified by the behavior of a State and by its ability to properly maintain its separate existence.

"Right" of independence

The "right" of independence does not mean that States are truly independent of each other. It merely means the right to a separate existence, the possession of a distinct international personality.

The "right" of sovereignty with reference to both the external and the internal freedom of will of a State has no real significance apart from the idea of independence. *"Right" of sovereignty*

The "right" of equality is evidently nothing more than the claim of nations to an equal right of recognition, and to the respect due them as separate political personalities. It belongs rather in the realm of international etiquette than International Law. As an alleged principle of law it is essentially unsound and dangerous, a step backward, an obstacle in the way of international order and organization. Liberia and Haiti might well be cautioned not to stress too urgently their claims to what the American Institute of International Law has seen fit to characterize as "the separate and equal station to which the laws of Nature and of Nature's God entitle them." *"Right" of equality*

In conclusion, therefore, it must be reiterated that rights spring from the legal recognition of definite interests. The Rights of States cannot be based on assumptions, on abstractions, on "fundamental postulates." No true system *Rights spring from recognition of interests* of law can be erected on so false a basis. It must be based on solid realities, on genuine interests definitely recognized and legally protected.

<small>International Law based on realities</small>

Whatever may have been the services of political theorists in behalf of the general rights of man, it would seem clear that International Law cannot now fall back on mere theories. Its most ardent champions have rendered it poor service in recent times by appeals to natural law and "absolute rights." It will never be entitled to full respect as a comprehensive, rational system of law until we have the courage to undertake anew to lay its foundations on the firm basis of international realities.

CHAPTER IV

THE LIMITATIONS OF ARBITRATION

We have heard much in regard to the limitation of armaments, but very little concerning the limitations of Arbitration. There have been hardly any limitations to the claims of extreme Pacifists concerning the sovereign merits of Arbitration as a substitute for armaments. Many hold with Norman Angell that wars do not pay—a most materialistic point of view for idealists to hold; that "there never was a good war or an honorable peace"; and that there is no reason why a nation, any more than an individual, should refuse to submit vital interests and questions of national honor to Arbitration.

Claims of extreme Pacifists

In their unbounded confidence in the efficacy of Arbitration as a panacea for international ills, however, the peace extremists have proved too much. In showing that Arbitration is a very ancient institution which has frequently been used by many nations, they have unconsciously drawn attention to the fact that it

Ignorance of Arbitration

must have decided limitations if nations in so many instances have preferred the arbitrament of the sword for the settlement of their disputes. The question naturally arises why this should be so. It is not at all satisfactorily answered by the general assertion that most wars have occurred because of the absence of an organized public opinion opposed to war. Apart from the injustice of denouncing statesmen burdened with the painful responsibility of accepting war in the maintenance or defense of national rights, this point of view reveals an inaccurate analysis of the causes of war. Failing to estimate with precision the exact causes of war, it is of course natural that these extremists should fail to comprehend the real functions and the scope of Arbitration as an alternative of war.

Causes of war

A proper understanding of the causes of war is not to be had through abstract theorization, but through a careful analysis of concrete examples. We need scientific laboratory investigations, not philosophical generalizations. If there are international ills to be eradicated, they should be correctly diagnosed and scientifically treated. They cannot be conjured

THE LIMITATIONS OF ARBITRATION 77

away by sentimental appeals, or by denouncing the horrors of war. And yet, during the past twenty years of peace agitation and arbitration propaganda, there has been manifested an extraordinary disinclination to learn even the lessons so strikingly taught in the six wars which have occurred since the Czar in 1897 issued his famous appeal for disarmament. The horrors of modern warfare are so unutterable that many sensitive persons are apparently quite incapable of finding a rational explanation of the causes of war. To such persons war is the abandonment of reason; it is the reversion of man to primitive savagery. They cannot see that, just as with bodily ailments, there may be specific causes of international ills; that, as in the community, where gross injustice prevails, there discontent and violence are likely to occur. When every other expedient to keep order and administer justice fails, there force of necessity becomes the *ultima ratio*. By those, however, who, like the physician, are able to ignore the horrors of war and disease, the brute, crude causes of war may readily be comprehended. A brief survey, therefore, of these recent Twentieth Century wars will be most suggestive.

Spanish-American War

The blowing up of the United States Battleship *Maine* in the harbor of Havana may have been the occasion for the war with Spain in 1898; it certainly was not the fundamental cause. Whatever the occasion and the causes of this war, one thing is clear: it put an end to decades of suffering and intolerable wrong, and resulted in what has been well termed "the abatement of an international nuisance." The questions involved were of such a nature that Spain could not possibly agree to submit them to Arbitration. They obviously could not be settled through Diplomacy. The assertion that Diplomacy might have found a peaceful solution is after all a mere conjecture; and conjecture of this kind, in the face of the failure of Diplomacy, would seem peculiarly futile. Whatever may have been the conscious motives of the American people in taking up the sword against Spain, in responding to the call of apparent duty, the results in Cuba, Puerto Rico, and the Philippines would seem to offer their own eloquent justification.

South African War

The war in South Africa, with all its unpleasant antecedents—the Jameson Raid and the Chamberlain-Kruger negotiations — seemingly performed the greatest beneficial service for both the Dutch and the British. Whatever may have been the inordinate pretensions of the British settlers, this war settled once for all that those who participate in the upbuilding of a State are to be treated as equals, and not as menials. There was nothing to arbitrate. Legally the Boers were essentially within their rights to do as they pleased with the land they had conquered and the State they had founded. This bloody war, however, decided otherwise; and the results to-day in South Africa, where a united people under the leadership of Botha, the Boer General, are fighting loyally for the British Empire, offer the most effective argument in defense of the great conflict. The assertion of Norman Angell and others that the same results might have been attained by peaceful means in the process of time would seem in the light of the actual situation hardly worthy of serious consideration.

The Russo-Japanese War, which the cleverest diplomacy could not avert, directed attention to the consequences bound to ensue when the expansive economic forces of two great nations come into collision and ignore the just rights of other nations. There could be no

Russo-Japanese War

doubt concerning the sovereign rights of both Korea and China. Neither Japan nor Russia had legal rights in Korea or Manchuria. And yet International Law and Arbitration are of no avail in such a situation. An arbitral tribunal would have been absolutely constrained to deny to Russia and Japan any rights superior to those of China and Korea. Holding the views they did, neither of the great contending nations could have appealed with reason to Arbitration. Convinced as they were that vital national interests were at stake, they could in last resort only appeal to the arbitrament of the sword. As we contemplate the mysterious operation of great unseen forces in the affairs of nations, have we any right to assert that this dreadful war was brought on by the evil designs of irresponsible statesmen? Conscious at least of the limitations of finite wisdom, one should not lightly support so hideous an accusation. It would certainly seem clear that the Russo-Japanese War *did* settle something. A perfect understanding now exists between the two nations, and the former antagonists are now brothers at arms seeking together the settlement of another inscrutable problem.

It is extremely difficult, if not impossible, to attach much weight to the ostensible reasons alleged by Italy for waging war against Turkey in 1912. The true cause of the war seemed to lie in the intense conviction of Italian statesmen that territory in Africa, not essential to Turkish national development, was most essential to the development of Italy. Arbitration in such an absurd case would unquestionably have gone against Italy, as it would in the instance of Russia and Japan. It is true, of course, that the people of Tripoli as a conquered race were not benefiting by Ottoman rule; and that Italian rule promised a much higher order of economic and social development. No matter how much one may denounce this war of aggrandizement, it would seem as if we were again in the presence of strange, imponderable forces which vitally concern the evolution of nations. Here is presented the whole great problem of colonial empire, the question of the conflict between the rights, the needs, and the obligations of higher and lower levels of civilization. Have ignorance, inefficiency, defective notions of justice, low standards of morals and behavior, superior or even equal rights when in conflict with high standards of education,

Italo-Turkish War

efficiency, justice, morality, and general conduct? One should try to answer questions of this character before passing final judgment on Italy's course in its war of aggression against Turkey in 1912.

Balkan Wars Most typical and illustrative of the fundamental causes of war were the Balkan Wars of 1912 and 1913. The war against Turkey was undertaken by Bulgaria, Serbia, Greece, and Montenegro in defense of the right of men to group together in accordance with their ethnic sympathies, their economic needs and interests. This principle, so cynically flouted time and again by the European Powers, in professed adherence to the doctrine of the Balance of Power, had been most flagrantly violated at the Congress of Berlin, which deliberately aimed to prevent the realization of the nationalistic aspirations of the peoples of the Balkans. Too much blame has been placed on the Turks. In common with other nations, they of course have their heavy burden of responsibility. Their follies and their crimes cannot be extenuated. Any other nation, however, in the place of Turkey would have found it supremely difficult to thwart the natural ambitions of the different races in Turkey in Europe to be re-

THE LIMITATIONS OF ARBITRATION 83

united with their own kinsfolk. The Balkan War of 1912, therefore, in the face of the sardonic diplomacy of the European Powers, and the obvious impotency of Arbitration to deal with such a chaotic situation, was plainly inevitable; it was in fact too long delayed.

This war, with its sweeping conquests, seemed in a fair way toward reaching an effective solution of the great ethnic problems involved, when inordinate cupidity on the part of the Balkan States themselves, and malicious diplomatic intrigues from without, precipitated the lamentable conflict between the victorious allies. The entirely unforeseen adjustment that followed in the Treaty of Bucharest, in failing to respect this basic principle of ethnic and national rights, sowed the seeds of future dissensions and conflicts. Bulgaria, deprived of extensive areas populated largely by people of Bulgarian stock and sympathies, was impelled in 1915 to throw in its lot with the Teutonic Powers in the hope of winning back this territory. An autonomous Albania was created by European mandate, in professed respect for the rights of nationality, of such restricted size, resources, and population as to be incapable of an independent normal existence. Monte-

Treaty of Bucharest

negro, possessing a barren district less than a third of the area of Vermont, with a population of less than 300,000, which was originally placed in the grip of Austria, through the opposition of that same Power, was denied the possession of territory absolutely essential to its economic and social development. Serbia, long in danger of strangulation by Austria, hoped by the Balkan War not only to be reunited with those Serbs under Turkish rule, but also to find at last a way to the open sea. The fierce opposition of Austria, abetted by other Powers, succeeded in thwarting this most legitimate ambition, at least so far as the Adriatic was concerned. It is possible that as a result of the Great War of 1914, Serbia may be able to free itself from the clutches of Austria and find some sort of access to the sea. Certainly as regards the future of the whole Serb race, which was originally broken into fragments by European consent, it is not to be expected that the Serbs will ever abandon the hope of being brought together in one household.

The Great War

One may well hesitate at this time to attempt any analysis of the causes of the great struggle now going on in Europe, Asia, and Africa. The complexity and the magnitude of the various

THE LIMITATIONS OF ARBITRATION 85

factors involved in the diplomacy preceding the outbreak of the war in August, 1914, afford ample opportunity for speculation and discussion. Two main truths, however, would seem to emerge through the diplomatic mist and the smoke of battle. First of all, it should be apparent that, whatever the deep-seated causes of the war may have been, they were not of a character suitable for Arbitration. To touch merely on one phase of the situation, Austria did not fail to make it perfectly clear that it could never submit to Arbitration its grievances against Serbia. Rightly or wrongly, Austria was evidently convinced that it must take its own measures of redress and protection for the welfare of the Dual Monarchy. Arbitration in this particular instance, as well as in the general broad issues at stake between the European Powers, was entirely out of question. *[Arbitration not applicable]*

The second great truth revealed by the Great War is that there exists between the nations of Europe a profound divergence of views concerning international rights and obligations both in time of peace and war. Nothing truer or more discouraging has been remarked in regard to this conflict than the statement of *[Divergence of views]*

86 INTERNATIONAL REALITIES

Maximilian Harden, editor of *Zukunft*, to the effect that the neutral nations were generally against Germany, not because they have not been told the truth, but because *they do not think in the same way as Germans think*. Whatever the merits of Germany's contentions may be, we are face to face with this tremendously significant fact: the nations of the world are still very far from possessing that common conception of rights and obligations which is absolutely essential for the building up of International Law and the settlement of international disputes by Arbitration, or courts of justice.

Scientific treatment of causes of war

A dispassionate study of the wars that have occurred since 1898 should at least have the effect of convincing one that the causes of modern wars are not trivial, and that they must be explained otherwise than by charging a lack of intelligence or of decent sentiments on the part of responsible statesmen and public opinion in general. The ills of the body politic must be diagnosed and treated scientifically, very much as the diseases of the human body. Mental healing and suggestion may be of value, but in the treatment of international ailments, it is of slight avail where nations hold

THE LIMITATIONS OF ARBITRATION 87

fundamentally antagonistic views, and differ in mentality. Essentially similar methods must be employed in treating international disorders as in treating civic disorders. Something other than sentiment and superficial treatment is required. Drastic measures of the nature of surgical operations are not infrequently demanded.

Recent Arbitrations

Having considered in this cursory manner the wars of the past eighteen years, it is likewise instructive to consider briefly the principal arbitrations of the same period. Since the adoption of The Hague Convention for the Pacific Settlement of International Disputes in 1899, fourteen or more controversies have been submitted to Arbitration by nations who were parties to that Convention and to the amended Convention of 1907. These Arbitrations have been hailed by many as great triumphs for peace under the assumption that they removed just so many possible causes of war. A closer study of the facts does not tend to confirm this point of view. It rather confirms the impression that Arbitration is essentially limited in its scope and functions.

Pious Funds Arbitration

The Pious Funds Arbitration of 1902 concerned certain funds held in trust by Mexico and claimed by the United States in behalf of the Catholic Bishop of California. Involving as it did the interpretation of treaty agreements and also of a previous arbitral award, this question was peculiarly fitted for reference to Arbitration. It was in fact much better suited for arbitral adjustment than through diplomatic negotiations.

Venezuelan Preferential Claims

The Venezuelan Preferential Claims Arbitration of 1904 in regard to certain claims which England, Germany, and Italy had sought to collect by force was also admirably suited for an arbitral decision. Venezuela, unfortunately, was obliged to sign a *protocol* submitting these claims to Arbitration, framed in such form as virtually to authorize the tribunal to issue an award containing a lamentable recognition of the preferential rights of those nations which resort to force in the collection of their debts.

Japanese House Tax et al.

The Japanese House Tax case in 1905; the Mascat Dhows case of the same year; the Maritime Boundary question between Norway and Sweden in 1909; the Canevaro Claim of 1911; and the Russian Indemnity question with Turkey of the same year, were all matters of relative unimportance, too technical in some

THE LIMITATIONS OF ARBITRATION 89

instances, and controversial in others, to be readily or properly settled by Diplomacy. Arbitration was therefore of special service in all these instances.

The incident at Casablanca, Morocco, in 1909, concerning the custody of a German deserter from the French Foreign Legion, though not in itself a sufficient cause for war, was one which might have furnished an occasion for war had either nation been so inclined. Neither nation was apparently inclined or ready for war, although considerably stirred up by this incident. It was accordingly referred to Arbitration with the result that the award assumed the nature of a compromise, an adjustment involving very little International Law and a good deal that was absurd. *Casablanca Arbitration*

So also with the Savarkar incident between France and England in 1911 concerning the custody of an Indian who sought asylum at Marseilles from the hands of British officials; and particularly the *Carthage* and *Manouba* incidents of 1912 between France and Italy in regard to French ships detained by Italian warships during the war with Turkey. None of these incidents were worth fighting over in *Savarkar Case*

North Atlantic Fisheries

themselves, nor were they worth acrimonious discussion. Arbitration was the easiest method available for the settlement of these annoying difficulties.

Much has been made of the North Atlantic Fisheries Arbitration between England and the United States respecting the rights of American fishermen off the coasts of Newfoundland and Labrador. As a question involving the interpretation of treaties and state documents, it was well adapted for arbitral decision. The wonder was that it had not long before been removed from the diplomatic table. The award, as Doctor Lammasch, the President of the Tribunal, remarked, "contained elements of a compromise."[1] It was, in effect, a conciliatory adjustment which recognized British sovereignty but allowed the main American contentions. Sir William Robeson, then Attorney-General for England, is said to have made the following significant commentary on the award: "We saved our sovereignty but cannot use it." The decision in this case, as in most Arbitrations, carefully avoided anything of the nature of judicial legislation. International Law cannot be said to have been increased or strength-

[1] *American Journal of International Law*, 1911, p. 725.

ened by the decision. On the contrary, in denying the existence of International Servitudes, the Tribunal ventured to annul a portion of International Law long accepted as analogous to easements under Common Law.

To be classed with Arbitration, in a sense, is the special Commission of Inquiry designated by England and Russia to investigate and virtually adjust the Dogger Bank incident of 1905, when a Russian fleet fired on innocent English trawlers under the fantastic fear of a phantom Japanese attack. Time is often the best ally of Diplomacy, and in embarrassing situations of this nature not worth bitterness of discussion or actual hostilities, Commissions of Inquiry serve a most admirable purpose.

Dogger Bank incident

In considering the various wars and Arbitrations since 1898, it is also very suggestive to bear in mind certain diplomatic adjustments of the same period, when Arbitration was unavailable because of the nature of the questions at issue, and war was possible of avoidance. In 1899, for example, Germany, England, and the United States reached a definite agreement in respect to the partition of the Island of Samoa, after years of diplomatic discussions and tem-

Recent diplomatic adjustments

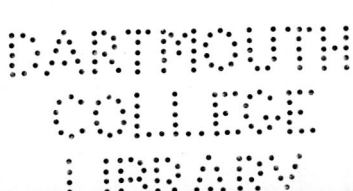

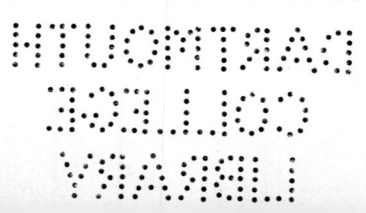

porary arrangements. England and France in 1904, after long years of distrust, rivalry, and bitterness culminating in the famous Fashoda incident of 1898, were able to effect an entire settlement of all outstanding differences. By this arrangement, France, among other things, received a free hand in Morocco in return for a recognition of England's interests in Egypt. In a similar manner, England and Russia put an end to their ancient and bitter antagonisms, in 1907, by coming to a general understanding which included the virtual partition of Persia, as well as other matters of vital importance. There have been other agreements between France and various Powers in regard to Morocco. Germany, as a result of its spectacular protest at Agadir in 1912, received a large piece of French territory in Central Africa, in return for the relinquishment of her pretensions in Morocco, while Spanish claims were satisfied by the cession of the Northern part of that country. Both of these agreements put an end to extremely embarrassing and threatening situations. It is of special interest to note also that, according to information of a trustworthy character from both British and German sources disclosed since the outbreak of the Great War in 1914, Germany and England had already arrived at an agreement in principle concerning their respective interests in Turkey and Persia.

In all these instances the questions settled by diplomatic agreements, relating as they did to the territory and rights of other States, were entirely unsuited for Arbitration. Though conducing for the time being to the general peace of Europe, such arrangements have been characterized, in part, by a frank disregard of the precepts of International Law, and the interests of other nations, weaker, and less advanced in civilization. Questions of this kind, it should be conceded, are mainly of a political nature as affecting conflicting national interests, whether just or unjust. They are not essentially judicial, admitting of the application of known principles of law by authorized tribunals. Nor is there an international legislature empowered to settle such controversies. They must therefore either be decided by diplomatic agreements, or by recourse to war, if the interests at stake so warrant. *[Nature of adjustments]*

From a rapid survey of the wars, Arbitrations, and diplomatic settlements of the last *[Conclusions]* eighteen years, it would seem that we are justified in drawing the following conclusions in regard to the scope and the functions of Arbitration.

I. Causes of war not trivial

I. It is evident that nations no longer go to war for trivial reasons, such as, for example, the gratification of the ambitions of irresponsible monarchs. They resort to the arbitrament of the sword only over questions vitally affecting their existence as international entities, questions which no one else has the right to determine.

II. War a last resort

II. Nations go to war only when Diplomacy fails, and Arbitration, because of the nature of the questions at issue, is quite impotent to find a solution, or impose its award. Where the rights may be entirely on one side, there is naturally nothing for the other to defer to Arbitration. So, likewise, there can be no Arbitration where nations arbitrarily decide the fate of third nations, such as Persia and Morocco, for example.

III. Arbitration for unimportant matters

III. Nations resort to Arbitration as a rule only in those cases which, though sometimes offering plausible pretexts or occasions for war, ns are not in themselves worth fighting over, and are too troublesome for Diplomacy to adjust.

IV. Nations resort to Arbitration not for purposes of strict justice, but for an impartial, conciliatory adjustment of conflicting claims. Arbitral tribunals have not the functions or the powers of courts of justice. This is due primarily to the absence of international statutes defining rights and obligations, and imposing penalties for wrong-doing. Furthermore, there is no feasible means for the enforcement of arbitral awards, and consequently arbitral tribunals are extremely cautious in their decisions not to penalize severely. They also wisely refrain from anything savoring of judicial legislation. The exact powers and functions of arbitral tribunals are not determined by a general law, or usage, but by the *compromis*, the specific agreement submitting a given controversy to Arbitration. This *compromis*, or protocol, even ventures at times, as in the case of the *Alabama*, to prescribe the law to be applied. Judges in real courts of justice would never consent to restrictions on their freedom of judgment with due regard for usage, precedents, and the ends of justice itself. At the present stage of international development, true courts of justice are not yet attainable for the determination of all litigation between nations. It is therefore an inexcusable confusion of terms to speak of the "Court of *Arbitral Justice*" proposed by The Hague Conference of 1907. The designation itself suggests somewhat the doubtful nature of Arbitration. Questions, therefore, which have been rather loosely characterized as "justiciable" in their nature, that is to say, which may be determined in accordance with the principles of law and equity, should not properly be the subject of arbitral decision. If submitted to Arbitration, the *compromis* of submission should be most careful to formulate the principles of law on which the tribunal should base its decision. Otherwise, it is quite certain to seek a conciliatory adjustment of the difficulty, not of a "justiciable" character. It is for reasons of this nature that we are justified in the conclusion that nations do not resort to Arbitration for purposes of strict justice, fully prepared to submit to all its rigors and penalties. Arbitration is generally invoked within restricted limits for the purpose of obtaining an impartial, conciliatory adjustment of conflicting pretensions.

THE LIMITATIONS OF ARBITRATION 97

V. Except in certain questions involving the interpretation of treaties and other written agreements, the arbitration protocol practically determines in advance, as in the Venezuelan Preferential Claims, or the *Alabama* Claims, the exact lines along which the decision is to be reached. This, of course, means that Diplomacy has already approached very near to a settlement, the exact terms of which are to be left to the judgment of the arbitral tribunal, the "compositeur aimable." Greater honor is therefore due in such instances to those who draft the agreement for Arbitration than to Arbitration itself.

V. Arbitration triumph for diplomacy

VI. Finally, viewed in the light of all that has preceded, Arbitration, far from being a general panacea for all international ills, is to be considered chiefly as an adjunct, an auxiliary of Diplomacy. Limited in its scope and functions, it is to be regarded, together with Commissions of Inquiry, as a welcome and valuable helpmeet in times of need and special stress. In the process of time, *pari passu* with the evolution of International Law and international polity, Arbitration may increase in usefulness and take on more and more of the character of a court of justice. But in the

VI. Arbitration the helpmeet of diplomacy

meantime, the advocates of the pacific settlement of international disputes would do well not to discredit Arbitration by placing on it a greater burden than it is yet able to bear. We should frankly recognize that it is still a very imperfect instrument. In our impatience for the realization of "the perfection in international relations," which Lorimer states to be the true object of the law of nations, we must continually remind ourselves that "the substitution of law for war" is a slow, laborious process. It is an inspiring task calling for great patience, courage, and faith.

CHAPTER V

INTERNATIONAL ADMINISTRATION

James Lorimer, that vigorous and most stimulating Scotch publicist, treating of the question of world organization, remarked more than thirty years ago that:

World organization

> The great impediment (in the way of the growth of international jurisprudence) . . . is the hopelessness caused by the *débris* of impossible schemes which cumber our path, and from these it must be our first effort to clear it.[1]

Among the "impossible schemes" must probably be included Lorimer's own earnest attempt to solve this great problem which he characterized as the "ultimate problem of international Jurisprudence."

Lorimer's scheme

Starting with the assumption that international order is to be secured in very much the same way as national order, he says:

> Savages are incapable of municipal organization beyond its most rudimentary stages; yet it is by means of municipal organizations that men cease to be savages.[2]

[1] *Institutes*, II, p. 197.   [2] *Ibid.*, p. 191.

100   *INTERNATIONAL REALITIES*

Following out the logic of his uncomplimentary analogy between nations and savages, Lorimer reaches the conclusion that an international legislature, judiciary, and executive are required to secure that order and freedom among nations which he holds to be the aim of International Law. Candor compels him to admit that "progress in the direction of the ideal by means of mutual aid, regulated by positive law, though possible within the state *may* be impossible beyond it; the ultimate problem of international jurisprudence, while demonstrably inevitable, may be demonstrably insoluble. The science of jurisprudence, when prosecuted in the direction of the law of nations, may end in a *reductio ad absurdum*."[1] Nevertheless, Lorimer has the courage to believe in an international administration of law comparable to the enforcement of municipal law.

Kant's scheme for "perpetual peace"

Immanuel Kant, presenting another "impossible scheme" in his memorable essay on "Perpetual Peace," also asserts that:

Nations must renounce, as individuals have renounced, the anarchical freedom of savages, and submit themselves to coercive laws; thus forming a community of nations

[1] *Ibid.*, p. 192.

(*civitas gentium*) which may ultimately extend so as to include all the peoples of the earth.

Kant is careful, however, to define his community of nations as meaning "a federation of peoples, but not necessarily an international state."[1] He furthermore concedes that:

> This juristic state must arise from some sort of compact. This compact must not be based, however, on compulsory laws like that lying at the basis of a state; it must rather be that of a permanent free association, like the above-mentioned federation of different states.[2]

It would seem that Kant, in his instinctive aversion to a universal state possessing coercive powers, revealed a better understanding of the facts of international existence than Lorimer. The trouble with many such attempts to deal with international problems is that confusion of thought must always arise whenever we try to reason by analogy between nations and individuals. This is evident in considering questions of honor, morality, and particularly so in treating of the international functions of the State.

Nations and individuals

In considering the problem of the international administration, we ought clearly to rec-

[1] *Ibid.*, p. 224. [2] Quoted by Lorimer in *Institutes*, II, 226.

ognize at the outset that nations do not meet together and intermingle in a community as do individuals. They do not merge their interests as "savages renouncing anarchical freedom." They do not agree on common conceptions either of legal or moral rights and obligations, choose their own magistrates, accept the rule of the majority; nor for mutual advantage submit to the benign rule of a common sovereign.

Municipal community

Individuals have every reason to come intimately together in the daily pursuit of a vital community of interests. Through their political organization they may secure ready and effective checks on the abuse of power by legislature, judges, and executive. As live, integral parts of a municipal organization, they can regulate, alter, abolish, and create anew the national state within which they have chosen to merge their interests.

International community

It is obvious that hardly any of this reasoning applies to international relations. The most that nations, jealous of their integrity, and conscious of their exalted missions, ask of each other is freedom to achieve their own worthy ends. That freedom is to be found in separate existence, not in a community existence: in a mutual recognition of each other's interests, not in submission to a common sovereign. They cannot possibly accept the idea of a *supra*national law imposing, as does municipal law, trying restrictions, complicated obligations, or punitive ordinances. The truth of this has been exceedingly well expressed by Reinsch, in urging the necessity of co-operative action between nations, when he says:

> Any attempt to urge states into action without a specific need, on the mere plea of the interest of internationalism, would be, in so far, to jeopardize the normal development and ultimate success of the great movement which is one of the most notable phenomena of the era in which we are living. Nor should we expect states readily to give up that power of self-determination, of freely selecting their means, methods, and activities, which constitutes the essence of political sovereignty; however essential, in their own interest, a participation in common action may be, they still remain the principal guardians of human rights and interests, and ought therefore to retain to themselves the necessary freedom of action which such a trust requires.[1]

The desire to convert International Law into *supra*national law arises probably from the Austinian concept of the need of a superior sanction to law, a concept which has obscured

International Law not like municipal law

[1] *Public International Unions*, p. 142.

the profound fact that the law of nations is of a distinctly different character from municipal law.

It may truly be affirmed that the *lex gentium* is of a more elevated nature. Applying as it does *inter gentes*, it does not appeal to the policeman; it appeals to reason itself, to the sense of equity, to a higher moral consciousness. It is based solidly on the Golden Rule interpreted in an imperative, utilitarian, and ethical sense, as enlightened self-interest. It is simply the recognition of mutual interests, of common legal rights and obligations. And the basic sanction of the law of nations consists in the consciousness of what Gareis has concisely stated as "anticipated advantages of reciprocity as well as fear of retaliation."[1]

Interests of nations

It would seem clear, therefore, that what is needed is not a sovereign international organization to create, interpret, and enforce law. The need is rather of a complete, just understanding between nations as to what constitutes their mutual interests.

International congresses

International congresses and conferences as adjuncts to diplomacy are greatly to be favored

[1] *Science of Law*, p. 288.

INTERNATIONAL ADMINISTRATION

in order to accomplish this great end. The functions of such conferences are of two kinds: one, political—and this the most fundamental—to determine the respective rights of nationalities in all that is essential to their free development; and the other, legislative, in order to formulate the law which shall safeguard these rights.

The establishment of an international tribunal as the supreme court of appeal when doubts arise concerning the interpretation of these laws is of course a logical necessity. It is by no means clear, however, that such a tribunal should possess coercive power, any more than in the case of the Supreme Court of the United States in controversies between States. *International tribunal*

It may safely be asserted as a general principle that any compulsion of a nation that does not appeal to enlightened self-interest may prove a grave menace; and where enlightened self-interest exists there is no need of compulsion. At any rate, in a normal state of international order established on a mutual recognition of definitely formulated interests, if a recalcitrant nation should need coercion or *No coercion of nations* chastisement, such an unwelcome task might better be performed through some such limited agency as an alliance of nations, whether openly avowed or in the disguised form of the proposed League to Enforce Peace. Power of such threatening proportions could never readily be intrusted by nations to the free action of a genuine international executive.

International executive impossible

If the preceding reasoning be accepted as sound; if we concede that International Law has no pretense to be *supra*national law; that it invokes no sovereign sanction, but appeals to the enlightened self-interest of states; then an international executive becomes unnecessary and even abhorrent. It would have a thankless task, and prove a constant cause of friction, a means of unjust coercion, a menace to national sensibilities and convictions.

Administration of International Law

The question naturally arises: how, then, is International Law to be efficiently administered? The answer, however, seems obvious; it is to be administered by national agencies. The courts of most nations are generally sympathetic to the law of nations. It is of pointed interest to note that even now, in the midst of this fearful war, the Supreme Court of the

German Empire should have seen fit to protect the patent rights of a French national actually fighting in the trenches in the defense of France!

When a court applies International Law as a part of Municipal Law there can hardly be any doubt as to the intrinsic value of that law. The difficulty is not in the nature of the law of nations, or in its enforcement. It lies in the failure of nations to formulate that law with precision, or to provide an adequate body of law covering the wide range of subjects which so often give rise to international litigation. *International Law "is law"*

This is particularly evident in that branch of International Law—which is truly an integral part—well characterized as Conflict of Laws. The grounds for these conflicts should be removed. The rights of aliens in their sojournings and wanderings as citizens of the world should be defined by mutual agreement. The rights of foreign creditors, for example, should be clearly determined. So, likewise, in regard to what may be termed international torts, where aliens are wronged by acts of the state. *Definition of rights required*

This great task remains in large measure to be performed through diplomatic agreements, conferences, and, if you will, through international legislation. The problem of the administration of this law may safely be left to national courts under the safeguard, in some instances, of an appeal to an international court.

There is no sound reason for believing that nations actually prefer recourse to war, or even to reprisals, in order to settle differences of a clearly justiciable nature. The present war has demonstrated all too eloquently the horrors, the awful cost, and the folly of litigation by force of arms. If the just political aspirations and national rights of states are satisfactorily gratified and determined, the serious grounds for international litigation by force will be effectively removed. This can be done neither by the imperious will of a conqueror, nor of an international sovereign executive. It can only be accomplished through mutual concessions, by the free will and consent of nations.

International administration

It may be thought that in eliminating the possibility of an international administration through the agency of a supreme executive, we have virtually excluded the possibility of any international administration whatever. But this is far from being the case. On the con-

INTERNATIONAL ADMINISTRATION 109

trary, a survey of the already existing agencies for international administration proves most suggestive and encouraging.

For example, the European Danube Commission has been of very great value in time of peace in the regulation of the international commerce of the states bordering on the river, as well as of other states represented on the Commission. *(Danube Commission)*

The administration of the Suez Canal in the time of peace has been of an international character, though as long as England controls Egypt it would be obviously a fiction to affirm that this waterway was truly internationalized. *(Suez Canal)*

Tangiers may properly be denoted as an international city, administered as it is by representatives of various Powers. Its situation, however, is quite abnormal, constituting a species of *modus vivendi*, in view of the conflicting ambitions of France and Spain, the Powers most vitally concerned. *(Tangiers)*

A most interesting problem awaiting solution at the outbreak of the Great War in 1914 was the disposition of the icy island of Spitzbergen, where the presence of coal deposits *(Spitzbergen)* has allured foreigners of various nationalities, and required the establishment of some form of municipal administration. It is understood that some such anomaly was agreed upon in principle, though the precedent of the *condominium* of Samoa by England, Germany, and the United States certainly does not augur well for the success of another *condominium* in Spitzbergen.

Constantinople

We are perhaps bound in this connection to speculate somewhat on the possibility of the internationalization of Constantinople and the two neighboring Straits. It may be conceded that an international administration by officials of some such nationality as the Swiss might prove feasible of organization and successful of operation. From the political point of view, however, such an arrangement could hardly satisfy in the long run the ambitions of Russia to hold in her own hands the best natural gateway to the Empire. The uncertainty that an international administration would be able, though willing, to effectively guarantee the security and the facilities demanded by so great an Empire, would doubtless constrain Russia to vigorously oppose any such arrangement. However that may be, if it be granted that

Constantinople and its approaches should be internationalized, such an arrangement would be necessarily of an abnormal, exceptional character.

Other abnormal forms of international administration are to be found in the foreign Sanitary Board and the Dette Publique of Constantinople. Imposed on the Turks to guard against dangerous epidemics, and to protect the financial interests of European investors, these two institutions, respectively, have been an affront to Ottoman national pride, and cannot claim a permanent existence. The Dette Publique, incidentally, raises the interesting question whether there should be an international bankruptcy law which would permit of placing an entire nation in the hands of receivers for the benefit of all foreign creditors, instead of in the hands of the loan sharks of one nation, which for political reasons may have encouraged such loans. The Sanitary Board, likewise, suggests the question whether nations should not be authorized to intervene in the affairs of any nation which may be criminally negligent in matters involving the health of neighboring peoples.

Sanitary Board, Dette Publique

Exterritorial countries

Other special instances of abnormal administration are to be found in the Mixed Courts of Egypt for the trial of cases affecting foreigners, and in the foreign settlements of Shanghai, Canton, and Tientsin. It is certainly of interest to note that in countries where exterritorial privileges still exist, foreigners have found effective ways, even while their respective nations are at war, to administer their common municipal settlements, and adjudicate their legal differences. Such arrangements, however —it must be repeated—can only be regarded as temporary and exceptional in character.

International Unions

Of much more vital interest and significance from the point of view of international administration are those numerous and highly important organizations known as Public International Unions which have to do with such matters as Communication, Economic Interests, Sanitation, Police Powers, Scientific and other purposes.

These unions may be characterized as non-political and non-lucrative, as opposed to alliances or commercial undertakings. A mere enumeration of certain of these agencies is most suggestive. The Telegraphic Union, The Universal Postal Union, The International

INTERNATIONAL ADMINISTRATION

Union for the Protection of Industrial Property, Work of Literature and Art, The International Red Cross, all of which have their home in Switzerland, have been accomplishing most beneficial results in their special fields. There are also the Metric Union in Paris, the Agricultural Institute in Rome, the International Maritime Office at Zanzibar for the suppression of the slave-trade, the Permanent Office of the Sugar Convention, the International Office of Customs Tariffs, and the Interparliamentary Union at Brussels. Of a distinct character and importance is the Bureau of Arbitration at The Hague.

When one considers the wide range of subjects of so great importance to the peoples of the different nations, the imagination is stirred with the possibilities of such agencies for purposes of international administration. In just such normal, reasonable ways are the peoples of the earth best able to advance their common interests and facilitate that mutual understanding which must lie at the very base of International Law. In a similar way the unlimited array of scientific, literary, religious, industrial, economic, and other societies organized between nations will also contribute

Service rendered by unions

incalculably to the breaking down of prejudices and the "perfection of the relations between states," which, according to Lorimer, is the true purpose of International Law. Diplomacy and law itself are spared considerable strain and friction by the creation of all these agencies.

International clearing-house

The most interesting and pregnant suggestion has been put forth to the effect that a central international bureau might well be established in some such Olympic precinct as Switzerland, to serve as the home of all the various public international unions, a kind of supreme "clearing-house" for these and many of the other societies and organizations having a non-political, non-lucrative purpose. Such a suggestion would seem to offer the most fruitful possibilities from every point of view as a practical means of helping on the cause of international solidarity.

Pan-American Union

An international "clearing-house" which has in it the elements of great promise is the Pan-American Union in Washington. Here centre the interests of twenty-one American republics. If Canada could find the way to come in, this Union would comprise virtually the whole of the Western Hemisphere, a world in itself, set apart from the troubled worlds of Europe, Asia, and Africa.

It is true that the Pan-American Union as yet possesses little power of an administrative nature. Nevertheless it exists as a tangible utterance of an ideal that may ultimately be realized. There do not seem to be any insuperable obstacles in the way of conferring increased powers on the Union to at least discuss questions of mutual interest to the nations concerned, or to recommend legislation or action which their relations may demand. It is quite conceivable that the Union might even be given legislative power to enact, *ad referendum*, regulations and laws on specified topics such as intercommunication, trade, industry, and other questions of a like character. Here might gradually be centred the routine administration of many matters, very much as is done now through the various international bureaus established in Switzerland.

It is possible, of course, that such an organization through the natural accretion of administrative powers might take on something of the character of an international executive. Whatever might be its ultimate evolution, by serving as a general "clearing-house," a central common forum for discussion, suggestion, or even legislation, the Pan-American Union would certainly prove of immense service in achieving some degree of international organization in at least this portion of a distracted world.

<small>Summary</small>

By way of summary, I have endeavored to establish in rough and cursory outline the following points:

(1) There is no true analogy between international and municipal problems. Though nations must need have recourse to war at times, they are not "savages." The ends sought by individuals within a community are very different from the ends sought by nations within the community of nations.

(2) International Law is quite distinct in character from municipal law. It is truly *inter*national, and not *supra*national. It does not appeal for its recognition and enforcement to a sovereign authority. It appeals to the sanction of enlightened self-interest, to "anticipated advantages of reciprocity as well as fear of retaliation." Its enforcement must necessarily lie with national agencies, though allowing for appeals in certain instances to

some kind of authoritative international tribunal.

(3) The great need is, not of a sovereign enforcement of the law of nations, but of a much more comprehensive and definite formulation of that law. A clear understanding of the mutual interests of states which it is the object of the International Law to protect is urgently required.

(4) Diplomacy and international conferences can accomplish in the main the great task of determining the rights and obligations of states, and of providing the law which should apply in controversies and litigations involving these rights and obligations.

(5) Nations cannot jeopardize the freedom necessary for the achievement of their separate purposes and ideals by submitting to a common sovereign possessing coercive powers. An international executive thus becomes undesirable and repugnant, a menace to the legitimate aims and sensibilities of nations.

(6) If an international executive is undesirable, there exist, however, other agencies of great importance for purposes of international administration. The Universal Postal Union with its headquarters in Switzerland is an ex-

cellent example. By utilizing and perfecting these agencies by providing a central international "clearing-house" for the many non-political, non-lucrative interests of nations—the Pan-American Union, for example—international solidarity may be most effectively attained. In like manner the encouragement of international societies and congresses covering the entire field of human interests will be of immeasurable aid to the great cause of internationalism.

Conclusion

In conclusion, therefore, we would do well to consider whether, in our anxiety to accomplish something definite for the cause of world peace, it would be wise to attempt the creation of new international agencies. Would it not be prudent to follow Lorimer's injunction against "impossible schemes," and to avoid his example by adding no more "*débris*" in the pathway of international jurisprudence?

We cannot presume to foretell or anticipate the destinies of nations. A world state may yet evolve. We are not concerned, however, with remote events of a problematical, speculative nature. Our immediate duty would not appear to impose the creation of a perfect scheme of world organization. Does it not rather consist in the utilization and perfection of the agencies already at hand?

CHAPTER VI

IGNOMINIOUS NEUTRALITY

Munitions embargo

The agitation for an embargo on the exportation of munitions of war from the United States has obviously been partisan in character, in order to offset the advantage obtained by England and her Allies through the control of the seas. It should also be apparent that it would be unneutral on the part of the United States to modify its attitude so completely in the midst of this war. It cannot, indeed, pretend to adapt its attitude to the varying fortunes of war. Nevertheless, the question of the sale of munitions of war by neutral persons to belligerents is of very great interest, in the larger questions it raises concerning the nature and obligations of neutrality.

United States vs. Great Britain

It should be remembered that the United States once complained that "England was the arsenal of the Confederates, from whence they drew their munitions of war, their arms, and their supplies." While it was admitted that

IGNOMINIOUS NEUTRALITY

neutrals might properly trade in military supplies in the ordinary course of commerce, it was "asserted with confidence that a neutral ought not to permit a belligerent to use the neutral soil as the main, if not the only base of its military supplies, during a long bloody contest, as the soil of Great Britain was used by the insurgents" (Geneva Arbitration).

It will be recalled that during the Franco-Prussian War, Prussia also complained through its Minister to the Court of Saint James, Count von Bernstorff, "because the English Government authorized the wholesale forwarding of arms to France, and thus practised a neutrality, not of a benevolent character, but of a character prejudicial to the interests of Germany, although Germany waged a war for a cause which England herself should consider as just."[1]

Germany vs. Great Britain

We now have another Count von Bernstorff, son of the Prussian Minister who presented this complaint to England, in the midst of a war of tremendous significance, presenting a similar argument on behalf of Germany, though, curiously enough, there is no attempt

Germany vs. United States

[1] *State Papers*, LXX, p. 73.

to persuade the United States of the justice of Germany's cause.

The essence of this argument is to the effect that "the United States is building up a powerful arms industry in the broadest sense"; that "this industry is actually delivering goods only to the enemies of Germany"; that "if it is the will of the American people that there shall be a true neutrality, the United States will find means of preventing this one-sided supplying of arms."[1]

American rights

In view of the clear and entirely convincing manner in which the United States has demonstrated the technical right of neutral merchants to sell munitions of war to belligerents—notably in Secretary Lansing's forceful reply of August 12, 1915, to representations of the Austro-Hungarian Government on this subject—there would seem to be no further need of argument. The technical rights of neutral merchants to engage in this commerce are not questioned, as admitted by Germany in the statement that "The German Government have not in consequence made any charge of a formal breach of neutrality."[2]

---

[1] German Minister for Foreign Affairs to Ambassador Gerard, February 16, 1915.

[2] Memorandum of German Embassy, April 4, 1915.

IGNOMINIOUS NEUTRALITY

The serious question raised is of much wider import. As Germany well says: "It is necessary to take into consideration not only the formal aspect of the case, but also the spirit in which the neutrality is carried out." We are bound to re-examine in a critical spirit the whole problem of neutrality, its fundamental basis, its exact nature, its alleged rights and obligations. *[Nature of neutrality]*

The supplying of munitions of war on a large scale to belligerents vividly suggests some of the extraordinary inconsistencies, the preposterous anomalies involved in any attempt to remain strictly neutral in a great world war.

Among these anomalies is the fact that while it is generally conceded that a neutral nation may permit private trade in munitions, it is not permissible to sell ships of war. The distinction between arms and ships, the one for ultimate use, the other for proximate use in warfare, is somewhat too refined for ordinary common-sense forms of reasoning, or for what has been well termed "the rough jurisprudence of nations." So, likewise, is the distinction which permits the exportation of military aeroplanes, or submarines in parts, though forbid- *[Ships and arms]* ding the sale of vessels ultimately destined for warlike use.

Definition of munitions

Another extraordinary phase of this question is the difficulty of defining munitions of war. As a matter of fact they are not merely arms and ammunition, ships and cannon. As Lorimer truly says: "They are what war demands, whether it is shot and shell, shoes and stockings."[1] . . . "All objects are munitions of war if a belligerent is in want of them; and no objects are munitions of war unless, or until, he is in need of them. Salt beef and saltpetre are precisely on the same footing in this respect; and steel bayonets may be a superfluity where steel pens are a desideratum."[2]

If provisions are more urgently required than arms to enable a belligerent to hold out and finally win, a neutral nation must naturally render a greater service by permitting such peaceful traffic than by the sale of ships and guns. The logic of such a situation would impose either a complete prohibition of trade between neutrals and belligerents, or no restrictions whatever.

Enlistments

Consider the matter of enlistments. A neutral nation is bound not to allow belligerents

[1] *Institutes*, II, 160. [2] *Ibid.*, 135.

to open recruiting agencies on its territory, but it is not bound to prevent its citizens from giving their services in various capacities to the belligerents. A neutral citizen may contract to provide arms and ammunitions, but may not contract to give his own services as a soldier, or engage the services of others.

Take again the question of loans, the supplying of the "sinews of war." They may be made publicly by belligerents on neutral soil; but public subscriptions and collections in their behalf are unneutral! Though a public loan may enable a hard-pressed belligerent to continue the war to a successful conclusion, it is quite an innocent commercial transaction, while the subscription is an unneutral service! *Loans*

In all these ways it is permissible for neutral countries to serve as the base of supplies, the "arsenal," the treasure-house of money and men, without being technically what Hübner calls either "a party or a judge" in respect to the belligerents.

But there are other anomalous aspects of this weird thing called neutrality. If a neutral nation may permit all these acts, it is still liable to serious interference on the part of belligerents. For example, neutral merchants *Rights of belligerents* may engage with impunity in the trade of munitions with a belligerent if their nation is contiguous to his territory; but such trade may be effectively prevented, the contraband confiscated, the vessel itself condemned, if found on the high seas. Moreover, while theoretically the neutral nation may claim the right to trade freely with the belligerents, it must be prepared to acquiesce in the rights of belligerents to institute complete blockades of ports, coasts, or —as would now appear to be the case—the blockade of an entire nation, the establishment of a stupendous siege.

When one considers dispassionately all these anomalies, these incongruities, these absurdities, even, of neutrality, he is constrained to challenge the very basis and nature of that abnormal institution, and to ask whether in a war of far-reaching effects and significance it is possible for any self-respecting nation to maintain a perfect neutrality or remain truly neutral.

The definition of neutrality as "a continuance of a state of peace" between neutrals and belligerents is obviously untrue in the light of the many restrictions which neutrals are bound to permit and the trying obligations they are bound to fulfil.

IGNOMINIOUS NEUTRALITY

Neutrality is by no means a normal state of affairs. It is essentially an abnormal relation based on a hideously abnormal state of affairs. War is the negation of law: *inter arma silent leges*. Litigation by force of arms, international disorder, the general disorganization of the community—all this, of necessity, places belligerents and neutrals in an entirely abnormal situation. As Lorimer soundly observes: "It is necessity alone which can justify either war or neutrality, and necessity is not a source of normal rights and duties."[1]

— Neutrality abnormal

War and neutrality being essentially abnormal in character, the next fact to be observed is the inevitability of a clash between interests of belligerents and neutrals. When nations are impelled to stake everything on the battle-field, to make the uttermost sacrifice, they must perforce look upon the interests of indifferent neutrals as of relative unimportance. Prudence, the military exigencies of the situation, as well as a decent consideration for others and for the rights of humanity, will naturally restrain belligerents from interfering as far as possible with neutral nations. But the brute fact still remains that the interests of

— Belligerent vs. neutral interests

[1] *Institutes*, II, p. 125.

neutrals, when they clash with the pressing necessities of belligerents in the throes of a tragic struggle, sink into relative insignificance.

Neutral rights uncertain

It is for these reasons that it is a thankless task to attempt to define the positive rights of neutrals: they are largely negative in character, varying with the nature of the contest. They are in the main such as the belligerents may choose to concede according to the issues at stake. This is why such a question as the lawful use of submarines is necessarily surrounded with so much uncertainty. This is why it was found necessary to organize the Armed Neutralities of 1780 and 1800 in defense of the alleged rights of neutrals.

War of 1812

The United States had ample opportunity during the Napoleonic wars to learn that the rôle of a neutral is exceedingly difficult. It will be recalled how England and Napoleon deliberately waged war on each other through neutrals; how skilfully Napoleon manœuvred the United States into war with Great Britain, when, as a matter of fact, we might with as much reason and better justification have gone to war with her enemies.

IGNOMINIOUS NEUTRALITY

And now history is repeating itself in a most remarkable manner. The United States finds itself directly and seriously affected by a war of greater magnitude and significance. Its interests are being interfered with by both sides, while one of the belligerents, in imitation of Napoleon's tactics, is avowedly employing drastic measures of retaliation affecting neutral interests, in the hope that pressure may be brought to bear on the other belligerent to modify its methods of warfare. The United States is thus again made to realize that neutrals must in some instances either endure considerable interference with their interests or else fight. The maintenance of neutrality under such conditions becomes increasingly difficult or well-nigh impossible. *Modern parallel*

Thus far we have been mainly considering the rights of neutrals; it is necessary also to bear in mind their obligations. *Obligations of neutrals*

The general obligation of a neutral is usually defined as non-participation in the contest. It must not allow its territory to be used as a base of operations—the improper use of wireless, for example—nor permit any kind of act which would indicate partiality. A fictitious impartiality which, under the guise of affording equal opportunities to all, really affords special facilities for the only side able to avail itself of the chance, as, for example, the use of French territorial waters by the Russian fleet during the Russo-Japanese War, is obviously not neutrality. The "benevolent" neutrality such as Prussia claimed from England in the Franco-Prussian War, though countenanced in principle by Grotius, is plainly a euphonism for unneutral neutrality.

Anything which renders a neutral nation of special service to a belligerent, particularly as a base of supplies, as an "arsenal"—to employ the term used by the United States in the Geneva Arbitration—is calculated to make it hated by the other belligerent. In other words, that nation which desires to remain neutral may find not only that its alleged rights are seriously violated, but that it is placed under an obligation of impossible vigilance to avoid appearing either as the "benevolent" neutral or the open partisan.

There are those who virtually ask, as does Germany in respect to the sale of munitions, that a neutral nation should alter its procedure and laws so as to redress the balance upset by the varying fortunes of war. This is asking the

IGNOMINIOUS NEUTRALITY

impossible. It was for this reason that the preamble of the Hague Convention of 1907 concerning the rights and duties of neutral Powers in naval war contained the provision that: "These rules should not in principle be altered, in the course of the war, by a neutral Power, except in a case where experience has shown the necessity for such change *for the protection of the rights of that Power.*"

Taking into account the basis and the nature of neutrality and the extraordinary difficulties in the way of its effective maintenance, it would appear that the nation which desires to insist on a free exercise of neutral privileges virtually finds itself reduced to the following alternatives.

Difficulties of neutrality

(1) Having no concern with regard to the outcome of the war, it would trade indifferently with both sides, thus aiding them to prolong the fight at its own profit. It cannot serve effectively to help end the contest. As Lorimer pertinently remarks, it "cannot strike up the swords of the combatants by putting swords into their hands, money into their pockets, or food into their bodies."[1]

(2) By reason of the ability of one belligerent

[1] *Institutes*, II, p. 135.

to control the seas, the neutral nation must find itself reduced to the rôle of supplying only one of the belligerents. Whatever it supplies, whether guns, food, or money, if greatly needed by the belligerent, will necessarily be of the nature of munitions of war. Under such circumstances it will not be strange if the other belligerent quotes reproachfully the words of Demosthenes: "That person whoever he be, who prepares and provides the means of my destruction, he makes war upon me, though he have never cast a javelin or drawn a bow against me."[1]

(3) If the neutral nation finds that its interests and sympathies are on the side of the belligerent which through the fortunes of war has lost control of the seas, it may find itself in the extraordinary situation of becoming the main support of the very side it desires to see defeated.

(4) If, however, its interests and sympathies are with the belligerent which controls the seas, the neutral nation may prefer to permit that side to place restrictions of perhaps a severe and unprecedented character even on its commercial intercourse with the other belligerent.

[1] Quoted by Phillimore in *International Law*, III, p. 404.

IGNOMINIOUS NEUTRALITY

In this case, if it tolerates under the thin guise of a benevolent neutrality technical violations of neutral privileges, it lays itself open to bitter and vigorous protests by the other belligerent against its patent failure to preserve strictly the impartial attitude of a true neutral.

Such, in brief, are the embarrassing alternatives which confront a nation in its efforts to preserve neutrality in the face of a world-wide war vitally affecting its own interests as well as those of the belligerents.

It would seem clear, therefore, in whatever light one regards neutrality, whether from the point of view of the rights of neutrals or the obligations of neutrals, that during a war of great proportions and significance a neutral nation must necessarily find itself in a most trying position. It cannot possibly escape some of the direct, as well as the incidental, hardships of war. When the family of nations is thrown into chaos, all its members must suffer in varying degree.

Under such circumstances, it must again be emphasized, a neutral nation may find itself goaded by its immediate or its ultimate best interests to take up arms. It must make cer-

True interests of neutrals

tain, however, that it fights for interests of general and fundamental importance, not for technical rights of a temporary or, possibly, doubtful significance. As a responsible member of the family of nations the neutral must be sure it does not follow a policy of unenlightened self-interest or shirk its duty to seek international justice and order. It cannot do this merely by a passive attitude of neutrality. It "cannot strike up the swords of combatants by putting swords into their hands."

Duty of intervention

It would seem clear that under modern conditions of easy intercommunication, of the intimate interdependence of nations, no great nation can affect a selfish indifference to the interests of other nations, whether in times of peace or times of war. The breakdown of international order must vitally affect every nation. The existence of international injustice, threats of aggression lust for territory, ambitions to restrict the freedom of others, contempt for the basic principles of International Law: all this must arouse any self-respecting nation from a state of callous indifference. The issues of a great war are of too deep significance for the cause of international order and world

IGNOMINIOUS NEUTRALITY

peace to permit of real neutrality. As Westlake so forcefully points out:

> There is no general duty of maintaining the condition of neutrality. On the contrary, the general duty of every member of society is to promote justice within it, and peace only on the footing of justice, such being the peace which alone is of much value or likely to be durable. . . . We may sum up by saying that neutrality is not morally justifiable unless intervention in the war is unlikely to promote justice, or could do so only at a ruinous cost to the neutral.[1]

Westlake's views

Lorimer, the great Scotch publicist, also deserves to be quoted in this same sense.

> When a question has arisen between two States, and, above all, when that question has led to war, the object of International Law is not to ignore the war, but to remove the cause which has led to it; and this involves giving to the question, not the cheapest and speediest, but the most exhaustive, and, as such, the most permanent solution. There may be cases in which that object may be, or may seem to be, attainable by neutrality or by intervention, indifferently; and in such cases an option between these two courses will, no doubt, be jurally open to the State which is unable to decide between them. But such cases must always be rare; and the acknowledged interdependence of states in our own time tends to render them rarer and rarer.[2]

Lorimer's views

[1] *International Law*, II, p. 161.   [2] *Institutes*, II, p. 125.

After emphasizing the undoubted tendency of all schemes for international organization and the maintenance of world peace toward intervention, Lorimer goes on to say:

> "Charity begins at home," and the real interests of his own country must always be the first consideration of the statesman; but to identify a policy of neutrality with the interests of international peace is one of the strangest hallucinations that ever took possession of clear-headed men.

Holding views of this character, it is not strange that Lorimer should find only two grounds of justification for a nation's remaining neutral: (1) "Involuntary ignorance, or intellectual and consequent moral inability to participate in belligerency"; (2) "impotence or physical inability to participate in war."

Neutral cannot be indifferent

It would seem as if Lorimer's statements were somewhat too sweeping, and fail to take into account localized wars between remote nations not intimately connected with other members of the family of nations, Bolivia and Peru, for example. The neutrality of Sweden in such a case would be fully justified. But, on the whole, it still remains true that there is an increasing realization of the interdependence of nations which renders their misfortunes and struggles of deep concern to each other. A remarkable manifestation of this tendency is the proposed "League to Enforce Peace." Viewed either as a kind of international executive or as a disguised form of alliance, this League is a bold enunciation of the duty of intervention to preserve peace. It is a frank abandonment of the idea of neutrality. It is an admission of the truth of Westlake's assertion that there is no duty of neutrality. It is a recognition of the fact that neutrality is usually ignominious.

By way of summary, then, the preceding considerations concerning the larger aspects of neutrality raised by the question of the sale of munitions of war by a neutral would seem to warrant the following conclusions: *Summary*

(1) Neutrality, like war itself, is entirely abnormal. It is based on necessity, which, as Lorimer points out, "is not a source of normal rights and duties."

(2) Belligerent interests take precedence over neutral interests. If a nation tries to remain neutral it finds it must suffer many restrictions and infringements of the rights of peace.

(3) It is impossible for a neutral in the varying fortunes of war to remain the friend of both

belligerents. It cannot alter its course according to the course of the contest. It cannot preserve a perfect neutrality. It cannot observe a "benevolent" neutrality and remain truly neutral.

(4) If a neutral nation does not wish to remain in a humiliating position it must be prepared to fight in behalf of its own best interests.

(5) If a neutral nation chooses to fight, it must be certain that it fights on the side of international order and justice.

(6) It is the positive duty of a nation as a member of the family of nations to actively assist in the maintenance of international order and justice. A neutral nation must necessarily become both a judge and a party in a world war. Its own best interests require that it should make certain that such a war ends to the advantage of the whole world. Mediation, abstention from intervention, indifferent neutrality are of slight value, or of no value at all. The self-respecting nation, capable of vision and sacrifice, and willing to play its part as a world-power, will not shrink from the cost and the dangers of intervention. Ignominious neutrality will be treated with just contempt as a refuge of a timid, selfish people, faithless to

their duty as responsible members of the great community of nations. They will justly deserve some of the scorn visited by Dante on "the angels, who were not rebellious, nor faithful to God, but were for themselves."[1]

[1] *Inferno*, III, 37-39.

CHAPTER VII

THE DANGERS OF PACIFISM

Pacifist propaganda

We are constantly warned of the menace of Militarism, but we hear very little concerning the dangers of Pacifism. Peace societies endowed with ample funds have bombarded the country with pamphlets, addresses, sermons, and articles in the press, trying to prove that the Great War was brought on by Militarism. We are told that war is irrational, ineffective, and unjustified; that international disputes are capable of settlement by peaceful means; and that nations should immediately disarm. Societies have been organized to counteract the movement in favor of a strong national defense. The gospel of military unpreparedness is being fervently preached in order to avert the menace of Militarism. Like the youth whom the poet counsels to bear a lily in his hand because "gates of brass cannot withstand one soft touch of that magic wand," we are counselled to go through this turbulent world of international politics without weapons of defense in order to demonstrate the purity of our motives!

It is not always easy to discover precisely what pacifists understand by Militarism. To some it signifies anything relating to armaments and armies; or it means *large* armies and armaments. To others it suggests large armies of the Prussian kind. Then again there are those to whom it connotes the political philosophy which believes in the efficacy of force to forward and protect the vital interests of the State. In general the pacifists unite in looking upon Militarism as a horrible monster that is more likely to control than serve the State. The Army and Navy are to be regarded as ever a potential menace.

<small>Meaning of Militarism</small>

If Militarism is vaguely understood, so also Pacifism is in great need of clearer definition. There are, of course, the extreme pacifists who hold that wars are never justified; that "there never was a good war or a bad peace"; and who agree with Norman Angell that wars never pay. They believe that war should be avoided at any cost; and that "peace and righteousness" are synonymous. There are other pacifists who fervently believe that in-

<small>Meaning of Pacifism</small>

ternational disputes can be satisfactorily settled by peaceful means; they have great faith in Arbitration, in courts of arbitral justice, and ultimately in an international police force. To such optimists all that is needed is a common agreement among nations to disarm, and abandon the "irrational" use of war. There is still another group of pacifists who believe that the peaceful settlement of international disputes is preferable to that of war, but are under no illusions concerning the defective character of the means of peaceful settlement now available. They are willing to aid in every possible way the cause of world-peace, but indulge in no sentimental notions in respect to disarmament. They see that international organization, like everything else in nature, is a process of slow evolution. They hold that the problem is mainly the stupendous one of "the substitution of law for war."

When we speak of the dangers of Pacifism, therefore, we do not have in mind this last category of pacifists; we have in mind those other pacifists who believe that war is never justified, and those who believe that adequate means for the settlement of international disputes are now at hand. It is not my purpose

THE DANGERS OF PACIFISM

to speak with scorn of the aims and accomplishments of these pacifists. The world has great need of idealists, even of the impractical variety. But idealists of the impractical variety may easily bring a good cause into disrepute and create a worse condition of affairs. It is therefore of immense importance, at this crisis in the world's history, that we turn for a moment from the denunciation of Militarism and try to consider in a detached way the possible dangers of Pacifism.

There exists a danger that Pacifism will discredit International Law by attempting to submit it to a strain it is not yet prepared to bear. Through a false analysis of the causes of war, a failure to understand world politics, and a complete misunderstanding of the nature, functions, and power of Arbitration, the pacifists are likely to bring International Law into disrepute. They do not seem to realize the crucial fact that there are questions of a non-judicial character which International Law cannot decide. If Diplomacy can find no solution, then war alone can decide questions of this character. *Pacifism expects too much of International Law*

Pacifists do not see that arbitral tribunals cannot indulge in judicial legislation where *Arbitration restricted in scope*

International Law may be defective. Odious as judicial legislation is in national courts, it is infinitely more so in international courts which by their nature cannot reflect common conceptions of rights and obligations. Work of this momentous character can be accomplished only by a properly empowered international Congress.

In exalting Arbitration as an efficient substitute for war, the pacifists do not seem to appreciate the fact that nations cannot refer disputes to Arbitration without restrictions on the exact powers of the tribunals. In the absence of an International Law enacted by common consent which may be confidently invoked in all disputes, nations are often compelled to prescribe the law and procedure to be observed in each arbitration. The *Alabama* Arbitration illustrates this fact. The protocol of submission practically settled the controversy between Great Britain and the United States. The triumph was one of Diplomacy rather than of Arbitration. If arbitral tribunals are not free to apply the law in each case, they are likewise not free to render decisions of a punitive nature, except to award damages in accordance with the protocol defining their powers. Nations would resort with extreme reluctance to Arbitration for purposes of punitive justice. Courts cannot punish unless they have a generally accepted law to administer, and have the power to enforce their decrees.

Arbitration as a helpmate to Diplomacy

It is not generally appreciated that Arbitration is essentially nothing more than a useful helpmate to Diplomacy. Nations go to war only over issues of vital importance which International Law is powerless to settle. They resort to Arbitration only over matters not worth fighting about which Diplomacy has been unable to adjust. The wars and arbitrations of the last fifteen years since the first Hague Peace Conference amply demonstrate this fact. In claiming, therefore, too much for Arbitration the pacifists are trying to put on it a strain it never was meant to bear. They are bringing International Law into disrepute by asking it to treat situations it is entirely incompetent to remedy, and the result is likely to be a discouraged reaction and cynical revulsion to redress of wrongs by force rather than by law.

In insisting too strenuously on its programme of Arbitration and disarmament, Pacifism has

146 INTERNATIONAL REALITIES

Arbitration propaganda embarrassing to Great Powers

aroused the distrust of the Great Powers. They are quite unwilling, naturally, to be placed in the embarrassing situation of appearing to foster ulterior ends of an aggressive character simply because they are unable to agree to arbitrate unreservedly all disputes or are unprepared to disarm.

European problems

American pacifists seem to forget that Europe has inherited from the Peace of Westphalia, from the Treaty of Vienna, from the Franco-Prussian War, from the Congress of Berlin, and other conferences distressing ills that the Great War may or may not remedy. It is possible that the map of Europe may be remade in accordance with the fundamental rights and the vital interests of all the various peoples concerned. A fine spirit of justice on the part of the conqueror may bring about results calculated to insure peace for many years to come. A bitter spirit of retribution, on the other hand, will surely sow the seeds of future wars.

America not mediator of Europe

American pacifists are in danger of seriously discrediting the cause of peace if they attempt in any way to bring pressure to bear on the European Powers and intrude as mediators in their political problems. These problems are of an intensely practical nature and must be solved by statesmen, not by impractical idealists. The United States must let Europe settle its own problems. The policy of non-intervention in the political affairs of Europe, as laid down by Washington, is an extremely prudent policy to observe at this crisis.

By stressing so insistently the subjects of disarmament and Arbitration, Pacifism is distracting attention and energies from the real work to be done. That task is the creation of a body of International Law to be formally accepted by all nations as the solid basis of their relations. It is futile to claim that such a body of law already exists. Apart from the Convention for the Pacific Settlement of International Disputes, the only convention creating law to govern the peaceful intercourse of States agreed upon by the Hague Peace Conferences of 1899 and 1907 was on the subject of The Recovery of Contract Debts. Consecrating as it does the vicious principle of the sanction of force in collecting debts, and accepted only with reservations by a considerable number of States, the value of this single piece of international legislation is extremely questionable. **Real task**

International legislation needed

Had the Hague Peace Conferences concentrated their efforts on the serious task of creating a law of peace rather than rules of war destined to be cynically disregarded under the plea of necessity, they might have materially advanced the cause of World Peace. Among the various international statutes requiring enactment may be mentioned the following: The rights of foreign creditors and the procedure to be followed in the prosecution of their claims. This procedure should be clearly defined. There should be an international bankruptcy law to govern the case where a State is unable to meet its external obligations. There is need of an International Law of torts to enable aliens to obtain damages for illegal acts of the State. The rights of aliens in times of civil disturbance should be determined by international legislation. There are also many questions classified under the head of International Private Law, or Conflict of Laws, such as marriage, divorce, guardianship, inheritance, and domicile, which should properly be regulated by international agreement.

Problems of Western Hemisphere

Questions of the foregoing character are of vital concern to the nations of this Western Hemisphere. If Europe has its own difficult problems to solve, America also has its own distinctive problems. If Pacifism would concentrate on this particular field of international politics instead of scattering its energies on vast world projects of a more or less chimerical character, it might accomplish practical results of great value. The pacifists in America would do well to encourage the creation of a body of law to govern the relations of the States included in the Pan-American Union, and thus eliminate many occasions for misunderstanding and estrangement. They might lead in a movement to transform the Pan-American Union into a congress empowered to deal not only with legal questions, but also to legislate concerning questions of a political character affecting the mutual interests of all. They might even achieve on this hemisphere the ideal apparently not within reach in Europe, namely, the establishment of a real Court of Justice properly supported by a Pan-American police force. Such are some of the practical tasks which Pacifism might help accomplish were it not so fatuously absorbed in the pursuit of impractical world projects.

Pacifism is fostering the spirit of cowardice and a materialistic conception of life. It has

Dangers of pacifism.

Pacifism fosters cowardice and materialism

stressed so vividly the horrors of war, has so effectively obscured the heroic, idealistic aspects of war, and insisted so strongly on the futility of war, that men are fast coming to believe that "peace at any price" is the best motto for a nation. It matters not what interests may be at stake, even independence itself; the great object of a foreign policy is to avoid war! For the followers of Norman Angell everything is reduced practically to a matter of material calculation. Wars never pay, they say. A thousand men must not be "sacrificed" to protect a hundred fellow countrymen in danger of torture and death at the hands of uncivilized ruffians. According to such a materialistic theory a man of genius should resist the impulse to save a drowning child because his own life is of greater value to the community. The chivalrous, self-denying, generous spirit is not to be fostered when men of one's own blood appeal for help from abroad! The peoples of the Balkans should never "sacrifice" lives for the sake of their brothers under foreign domination!

Pacifism ignores spiritual values

Pacifism has inculcated such an exaggerated conception of the value of life as to treat it as something immortal, something which must be

THE DANGERS OF PACIFISM 151

preserved. It is not something to be freely laid down in accordance with the precepts of Christianity! Surely this is to lose sight almost completely of the spiritual values. In failing to glory in the magnificent idealism of the soldiers of all the opposing armies now in combat who are joyfully giving their lives for something not themselves, who are inspired by a transcendent national ideal, Pacifism is leading the rising generation to worship at a sordid, selfish shrine. It is fostering a spirit of cowardice of a peculiarly abhorrent kind.

It is now the fashion among the pacifists to decry the spirit of nationalism as something narrow, provincial, and antagonistic to the growth of the sentiment of international friendliness. With Doctor Johnson they are disposed to regard patriotism as "the last refuge of scoundrels." They look with alarm on the recrudescence of nationalism throughout the world, and argue that international good-will and peace depend on the obliteration of national boundaries. This argument was much used before the present war by the Socialists and the Industrial Workers of the World, who claimed that the international solidarity of the working men of all nationalities would effectively

Pacifism versus Nationalism

prevent wars. Since the participation of the German Socialists in the aggression against their brothers in Belgium, however, this argument has had a considerably lessened value.

Nationalism misunderstood

In preaching loyalty to the rather vague sentiment of international brotherhood, pacifism would seem to fail to appreciate the true value of nationalism. It forgets that loyal devotion, like true charity, must first begin at home. One must show brotherly love to the man next to him, whether in his own home or his neighbor's, before he can talk about international brotherhood. The pacifists do not seem to realize that patriotism, like family loyalty, does not mean indifference to the interests of others. They err with the Socialists in ignoring the positive necessity of national units of organization in order to deal effectively with problems of education, religion, philanthropy, and economic administration. They also would appear to ignore the truth of the thought suggested by Lorimer:

> May it not be that under these diverse ethnical impulses diverse types of nationality must necessarily grow up, and that these, though permanently dissimilar, may be of equal ethical value with that which our ethnical genius has imposed upon us (Great Britain), and equally entitled

THE DANGERS OF PACIFISM

to international recognition by us and the other nations of Western Europe?[1]

Need of Nationalism

It would seem evident that the world has need of the free play of individuality among nations as well as among men; and that there is likewise the same need of mutual forbearance and respect. Pacifism, therefore, in belittling the sentiment of nationality, the loyalty of patriotism, is guilty of the grave offense of seeking to extirpate a sentiment capable of noble deeds, without supplying an adequate substitute. One cannot expect youths who are incapable of enthusiastic devotion to the State to render very much service to a vague, intangible World-State which has not yet come into being. Never was idealism so infelicitous as in this intolerance of patriotism.

Pacifism as a contributing cause of war

The severest indictment, however, to be brought against Pacifism is that it may be a contributing cause of war. The most tragic fact disclosed by the British White Papers in respect to the diplomatic negotiations leading up to the Great War is that Pacifism in England had practically paralyzed Sir Edward Grey's efforts in behalf of peace. When urgently pressed by Russia and France to make

[1] *Institutes*, I, p. 94.

clear to Germany that England would not keep out of a Continental war, Sir Edward was compelled to maintain a non-committal attitude which, as a matter of fact, was altogether inconsistent with England's obligations and interests. Pacifism had gained such a hold throughout England that the Government had neither the support of public opinion nor of the Liberal Party, until the actual violation of Belgian territory. Within the Cabinet itself were such strong and extreme pacifists as Lord Morley and Lord Haldane, the latter of whom after his visits to Germany was obsessed by belief in the force of international "*Sittlichkeit*," and the conviction that war between the two countries was "unthinkable." The undisguised surprise and fury of Germany on learning that England at the last hour was really determined to fight, is striking justification of the belief held by Russia and France that Germany would have avoided a general European war once it was clear that England would also be compelled to enter. The failure of Sir Edward Grey to make this fact explicitly clear to Germany must be traced, not to Machiavellian motives—as Shaw with ingenious effrontery would try to prove—but to the unwillingness

THE DANGERS OF PACIFISM

and inability of Englishmen to realize the imminent danger of war. This unwillingness and inability would seem clearly due to the insidious propaganda of such well-meaning idealists as Norman Angell and Lord Haldane. So infected had England become with the notion that war with Germany was as impossible as it was irrational, the pacifists were able to defeat the heroic attempts of Earl Roberts to secure an adequate military organization for the defense of the Empire.

Pacifism versus Preparedness

A peace society in America has circulated with evident approval the speech of a British member of Parliament in opposition to the increase of the British Army so eloquently urged by Earl Roberts. One would think that when this member of Parliament contemplates the fearful price England has had to pay for its military unpreparedness he would hang his head in shame and bitter remorse. Whatever the feelings of personal responsibility this member may have experienced, it is clear that many pacifists in America are willing to imitate his example, as is evidenced by their organizing a campaign of opposition to the movement to strengthen the arms of defense of the United States. Unable to understand the deeper causes of war, or to read aright the warnings of the present catastrophe, they hold, with arguments which defy ordinary standards of logic, that inasmuch as military preparedness failed to avert war in Europe, the United States should now try military unpreparedness! They insist that we should demonstrate the righteousness of our own motives by standing defenseless in the defense of Peace!

Conclusion

If it were simply a matter of demonstrating that Pacifism is in error in its fundamental premises and deductions, one would not need to feel any great concern. The world is accustomed and friendly to impractical reformers. But when Pacifism with the support of ample funds and influential leaders of public opinion is able to carry on a propaganda of such a nature as to constitute itself a contributing cause of war, it is something to be viewed with genuine apprehension. Statesmen are occasionally guilty of errors of judgment and criminal negligence in respect to the vital interests of the State. Responsibility can be definitely placed on them, and they have a heavy burden to carry to their graves. This is not true of the idealist who, lacking the steadying, sober

THE DANGERS OF PACIFISM 157

influence of responsibility, would attempt to manage the affairs of nations. With a disregard of consequences which would almost be treason on the part of statesmen, the idealist would willingly endanger the safety of his country for the sake of the problematical triumph of his ideals. It is earnestly to be hoped that the pacifists may be led to realize the dangers of their propaganda, and that the United States may be spared the terrible misfortunes which have come upon Europe.

CHAPTER VIII

PAN-AMERICANISM

Misdirected idealism

Since the Czar of Russia took the initiative in summoning the first Peace Conference at The Hague in 1899 the world has suffered from an almost unintermittent series of wars and revolutions. A dispassionate consideration of this turbulent state of affairs should cause the friends of peace to think soberly. We cannot, with justice or reason, be undiscriminating in placing the blame for these harrowing events. We ought now to be conscious of the fact that a splendid amount of idealism has been sadly misdirected. We have urged disarmament when nations knew that it was impractical, and that to do so would invite disaster. We have urged Arbitration, as a general panacea for international ills, when it should have been evident that Arbitration has its most decided limitations and is incapable of adjusting momentous questions of a political, non-judicial character. We have sought to establish courts of justice when there was little or no law for the courts to administer. We have pleaded for international order when there was no force to keep order. We have blindly accepted the intolerable international *status quo* with no thought of redressing the wrongs of outraged nationalities. We have considered peace as something tangible to be attained through agreement, and have failed to realize that peace is a state—a resultant of actual fluctuating conditions which in themselves, in last analysis, depend internationally, as within any community, on the intelligence, morality, and sense of justice of the average man.

The great definite task we have particularly ignored in our enthusiasm for world peace is that of peace and unity on this American continent. Statesmen like Blaine have realized the importance of this magnificent task. Many have spoken and written in favor of a "better understanding," of the "need of closer relations," etc., between the nations of this hemisphere. The Pan-American Union was organized for this specific purpose, and is now enthroned in a beautiful palace in Washington. But what is the practical result of all this agitation and

The American problem

organization? Not much more, it would appear, than flowery sentiment and the awakening of keener interest on the part of business men in openings for trade in Central and South America. Diplomatically, we seem hardly any nearer a closer union between the nations of this continent than twenty-five years ago. In some ways, we would seem further away, owing to certain incidents which have aroused mistrust and fear concerning the policy and aims of the United States. Particularly to be regretted are the attempts of "Dollar Diplomacy" under President Taft "to substitute dollars for bullets"; the Mexican policy of President Wilson, and his endeavor to define the Monroe Doctrine as something quite distinct from Pan-Americanism—as the unique possession of the United States, which permits us to exert a kind of moral, and even political, surveillance over the domestic affairs of the other Republics. They have been led to apprehend that they are not free to grant foreign concessions or change their Governments according as they may desire.

Failure of United States Pan-American policy

This brings us to a consideration of the main reasons why it is that the idea of Pan-American unity has failed as yet to attain any practical results. First of all—and primarily—the nations to the south have been unable to accept with enthusiasm the idea of Pan-American unity because of startling extensions and interpretations of the Monroe Doctrine. Originally accepted with gratitude and joy, this Doctrine has lately awakened keen distrust and fear. It has even been characterized as an "obsolete shibboleth," as utterly abhorrent to the peoples of these countries. They have understood it of late as an egotistic assertion by the United States of a right of hegemony, and of intervention in their affairs. So strong has this sentiment become, that there are clear indications of a desire to form alliances to counterbalance this apparent assumption of overweening lordship.

Secondly, there is a keen appreciation among these nations of the supreme need of the creation of a body of law to govern the international relations of the States of this hemisphere. Arbitration without law is, with reason, of little value in their eyes. From their point of view there can be no genuine unity worthy of respect that is not founded on common conceptions of rights and obligations. They realize better than ourselves the obstacles to be overcome in

Need of law between Republics

this regard. They ask not for leadership. They ask for equality before law. And they ask for law to which they have previously given their positive assent. Until that law and that equality exist, they refuse to accept the dictation of the United States, no matter how altruistic and disinterested that dictation may be.

The Monroe Doctrine as interpreted by Mr. Root

The first and the main obligation of the United States is either to abandon the Monroe Doctrine or to formulate it anew in such terms as will obtain the unhesitating adhesion and the enthusiastic support of the other States of the Pan-American Union. To abandon this ancient bulwark of independence would seem folly if the objections are not against the Doctrine itself, but are based, as would appear, on recent extraordinary misinterpretations of it. Senator Root, in his Presidential address at the Annual Meeting of the American Society of International Law in Washington, in April, 1914, came very close to formulating the Monroe Doctrine in terms which should be acceptable to all the States of this continent when he said:

> The Monroe Doctrine does not assert or imply any right on the part of the United States to impair or control the independent sovereignty of any American State.

PAN-AMERICANISM

In the lives of nations, as of individuals, there are many rights unquestioned and universally conceded. The assertion of any particular right must be considered, not as excluding all others but as coincident with all others which are not inconsistent. The fundamental principle of International Law is the principle of independent sovereignty. Upon that all other rules of International Law rest. That is the chief and necessary protection of the weak against the power of the strong. Observance of that is the necessary condition to the peace and order of the civilized world. By the declaration of that principle the common judgment of civilization awards to the smallest and weakest state the liberty to control its own affairs without interference from any other Power, however great.

The Monroe Doctrine does not infringe on that right. It asserts the right. The declaration of Monroe was that the rights and obligations of the United States were involved in maintaining a condition, and the condition to be maintained was the independence of all the American countries. It is "the free and independent condition which they have assumed and maintained" which is declared to render them not subject to future colonization. It is "the governments who have declared their independence and maintained it and whose independence we have on great consideration and on just principles acknowledged" that are not to be interfered with.

In the course of this address Senator Root also said: "The Doctrine is not International Law, but it rests upon the right of self-protection and that right is recognized by International Law. The right is a necessary corollary of independent sovereignty." It is true that Senator Root would restrict the scope of the Doctrine to the assertion of the right of the United States, or Brazil, or Peru, to adopt proper measures of self-protection that each might deem necessary. According to Mr. Root, it would have no communal significance. It would remain a declaration of national policy, not the assertion of a fundamental principle of International Law.

<small>The Monroe Doctrine a sanction of International Law</small>

It would seem, however, as if Mr. Root, in a natural desire to reserve liberty of action to the United States, was resorting to a nicety of argument not devoid of inconsistency. One may well question the alleged "right" of a state such as Morocco, for example, to exist, but once a group of nations have explicitly, or impliedly, conceded to each other a qualified, or unqualified, right of existence—as would seem to be the case on this continent—a declaration on their part to stand together in mutual self-defense would appear to be the most solemn assertion of International Law. Without accepting in all their possible implications Mr. Root's theories of "Sovereignty," the Monroe Doctrine in the light of his own definition would thus seem to provide on this continent a definite sanction of International Law that has been lamentably lacking in Europe, where the rights of smaller nations have been subservient to the archaic and cynical doctrine of the "Balance of Power."

It should, of course, be recognized that every nation must necessarily reserve to itself the right to liberty of action in certain situations of near-neighborhood interest, such as confronts the United States on its Mexican frontier. We should not confuse questions of this nature with the Monroe Doctrine itself. With this reservation in mind, we should be prepared to abandon the Monroe Doctrine as an arrogant assertion of national policy and restate it in broad general terms as the defense of a fundamental principle of International Law. There would then exist no reason why all the other nations of the Pan-American Union should not enthusiastically support this Pan-American Doctrine. We would have thus removed the natural mistrust and fear that the policy and acts of the United States have so unfortunately aroused of late.

The Monroe Doctrine a Pan-American doctrine

The creation of law

Having reached a broad understanding of this nature, we might then properly direct our attention to the tremendous task of creating the law to be applied in the mutual relations of the Republics of this continent. It is highly desirable, for example, that there should be an agreement defining the rights of international creditors, and prescribing the precise mode of procedure to protect these rights. There should be an international law concerning claims founded on government concessions granted to aliens, and international law defining the rights of aliens in times of domestic revolt, and an international law of torts to determine definitely the rights of aliens in claims for damages on account of alleged injuries at the hands of foreign states. Such questions of moment should never be left to the arbitrary caprice of governments; nor should they be carelessly submitted to Arbitration without any previous agreement as to the law to be applied.

International Private Law

There is also an immense amount of work to be done in the field of International Private Law in order to help bring the nations of this continent into closer harmony. In Europe very much has been accomplished by international conventions to obtain uniformity in law and procedure, and thus remove possible occasions for serious conflicts of law. These agreements relate mainly to commercial practice and to questions concerning "personal status." It is most desirable, for example, that the United States and other members of the Pan-American Union should come to a definite understanding with respect to the rights of domicile and nationality.

The task of removing possible grounds for conflicts of laws is rendered supremely difficult by reason of the two distinct systems of law in use in the United States and in the other nations of America, as well as by reason of the peculiarities of our constitutional system which in itself stands in the way of uniformity of law and procedure within the borders of the United States. And yet if the difficulties are great, they also indicate how great is the need of reconciling antagonistic conceptions of law, whether within or without our borders. The unity of nations must depend primarily on a harmonization of varying notions in regard to legal rights, duties, and remedies. If nations have no common law, if their fundamental conceptions of rights and obligations are in-

"Conflicts of laws" within United States

compatible, it is futile to ask them to have recourse to a common court of justice.

Commission of Jurists

The Third International American Conference of 1906 appointed a Commission of Jurists "for the purpose of drafting codes of Private and Public International Law regulating the relations between the nations of America." At the opening of the Congress of these jurists, held in Rio Janeiro in 1912, the representative of the United States, Honorable John Bassett Moore, summarized in the following comprehensive manner the work of the Commission:

> The duty of the present Congress is comparatively simple, and, as it does not embrace the discussion of principles or the conclusion of conventions on controverted topics, may no doubt be expeditiously performed. Our meeting upon the present occasion marks only the beginning of the great work that lies before us, a work that will involve hereafter the prolonged and profound study of general principles, of conventional agreements, and of domestic legislation and judicial and administrative decisions, to the end that by becoming acquainted with our points of disagreement, as well as of agreement, we may be sure of our ground and go forward with a precise knowledge of the actual legal situation in each country concerned.

It is earnestly to be hoped that this Commission of Jurists may be able to formulate special laws to apply in some of the instances previously mentioned, where everything is at present so confused and discordant as to constitute a constant menace to the peaceful relations of the American nations. The adoption of the recommendations of this Commission should not prove difficult or doubtful. One practical result of their labors in Rio Janeiro was the adoption of an agreement concerning the law and procedure of extradition.

Another most promising agency for the creation of the body of law needed for the harmony and welfare of relations of the American Republics is the International High Commission on Uniformity of Laws created by the First Pan-American Financial Conference held in Washington in 1915. Its object is to devise means of adjusting and harmonizing the principles and procedure of commercial law and administrative regulation in the American Republics, and to work for the solution of legal problems in the fields of banking and public finance. History, both recent and remote, should conclusively demonstrate that international harmony cannot depend on good-will alone, or on what Lord Haldane so lauded as international "*Sittlichkeit.*" It rests ultimately

[sidenote: International High Commission on Uniformity of Laws]

on the just recognition of mutual interests. There can be no international peace where these interests are not clearly recognized, duly respected, and legally protected. There can be no possibility of international organization until common understandings exist concerning the practical problems arising out of the normal intercourse of nations. There is perhaps a danger in exaggerating the influence of economic factors in history; but there can be no doubt that human affairs cannot be regulated by sentiment alone. The United States Constitution owed its inception to an unofficial conference of delegates at Annapolis to consider the mutual economic interests of the States of the Confederation. May we not reasonably hope that the labors of such bodies as the International High Commission on Uniformity of Laws, and the Commission of Jurists may prove the logical first steps toward an effective organization of the American nations which shall be based, not on sentiment, alone, but on solid interests clearly defined and protected by uniform legislation?

The Pan-American Union; its possibilities

This brings us to the consideration of a most important question, namely, the functions and scope of the Pan-American Union in Washington with reference to all matters of mutual interest, particularly the adoption of laws governing the relations of the States which are members of the Union. Is it not of great significance that during this momentous war the representatives of the Union should have been in constant consultation in respect to the protection of the rights of neutrals? Is there any sound reason why they should not be empowered to crystallize their common counsels into definite and permanent form as an integral portion of the international legislation of the American nations? If the affairs of any particular nation should become so utterly demoralized as to give serious concern to its neighbors, why should not this representative assembly be fully empowered to deal directly with the problem involved, or to delegate such power to certain of its members? If it should appear that the Republics of Central America would be infinitely better off united again in one state, and that they were awaiting only the sympathetic initiative of outside friends, what finer work for the cause of peace could the Pan-American Union accomplish than the reuniting of brothers suffering from the evils of disunion? Should we come to realize that one of the greatest obstacles to international peace is the existence of artificial economic barriers, erected at the behest of a benighted Chauvinism, could we not through the medium of the Pan-American Union attain an agreement to abolish protective tariffs and narrow restrictions on coastwise trade? Through the judicious use of the principles of initiative and referendum, it would seem as if we had in the Pan-American Union precisely the organization needed to effectively express, and practically to apply, the sentiment for unity already in evidence.

Duty of United States for peace

In the great movement for world peace, the special duty of the United States would therefore seem to be this most difficult, though inspiring, task of helping to bring into harmony the Pan-American nations. If we labor wholeheartedly to foster like conceptions of rights and duties, and identic economic interests and sympathies, then may we decide in common those large questions of mutual concern which are now left to the separate diplomatic negotiations and agreements of the several American nations. Then may we constitute a genuine American legislative assembly. Then may we lay the solid foundations of unity on the sound basis of law. Then may we look forward with justifiable optimism to the speedy establishment of an American International Supreme Court of Justice, maintained by an adequate sanction and thus worthy of all respect. But these magnificent projects will not be accomplished merely through a realization of their desirability or of their feasibility. "The substitution of law for war" is a painfully slow process. It is to be done by "doing the work that's nearest." And the "work that's nearest" for us is the splendid task of converting Pan-American Union into Pan-American Unity, based on positive law and true justice.

CHAPTER IX

DEMOCRACY AND DIPLOMACY

Causes of the Great War

Explanations of the causes of the Great War of 1914 are naturally diverse, varying with the prejudices, the temperament, and the type of mind of each individual. Some hold that it was caused by Militarism—a conveniently vague term, like Socialism. Others attribute the war to commercial greed, love of power, the mutual distrust of nations, or to the passions and evil hearts of men.

The "democratization of foreign policies"

An explanation readily accepted is that the great catastrophe is directly due to the intrigues, the machinations of Diplomacy. It is easy to picture Democracy as the helpless victim of designing Diplomats who take a fiendish delight in wicked conspiracies, and find their supreme satisfaction in provoking a world war. The popular cry now is for the abolition of "Secret Diplomacy," and the "Democratization of Foreign Policies," in the naïve belief that the people are quite capable of carrying on diplomatic negotiations in the market-place. Among the able exponents of this theory are Norman Angell, G. Lowes Dickinson—both Englishmen—and Walter Lippman, in his most interesting book, *The Stakes of Diplomacy*. They support their thesis with considerable dialectic skill, and brush away difficulties with an argument to the effect that things could not be much worse under a democratic control of foreign affairs—a kind of reasoning which would justify invoking the services of a veterinary surgeon in a case of appendicitis or cancer, when the skilled physician had not been able to effect a cure or obviate an operation.

At the outset it would seem desirable to note what seems to be a fundamental misapprehension back of this current distrust of Diplomacy, namely, a confusion of methods with policy. Diplomacy and its agents have been credited with possessing power they do not possess, particularly since the introduction of easy means of communication, which no longer, as formerly, permit very much personal freedom of action, initiative, and discretion. They are credited with being the directing force, when they are only the instruments, the agents. It

Popular confusion of Diplomacy with policies

is true that Diplomats intrigue at times, and resort to questionable methods to accomplish their ends; but so do lawyers, business men, politicians, and even representatives of philanthropic or religious organizations. One does not feel justified thereby in condemning the profession of law, business, politics, philanthropy, and religion. In many instances, if the firm, society, or organization find that their representatives are behaving improperly they are quick to reprove, punish, or discharge such unworthy agents. In other instances, if the directing policy of these organizations is found to be dishonest or vicious, criticism is properly centred not on the representatives, but on the management.

Statesmen determine diplomatic policies

And so it is with Diplomacy: the agents, the mere tools, are of slight account. The powers that direct, the policies they formulate, are the supreme factors. Foreign policies depend very largely on the character and intelligence of the statesmen responsible for the conduct of foreign relations. A Metternich, holding reactionary though honest opinions, will resort to methods hateful to Democracy. A Cavour, fired by nationalistic dreams for his country, will use various means at hand

DEMOCRACY AND DIPLOMACY

to achieve his worthy ends. So with a Gladstone full of moral zeal; a Bismarck seeking the unity of Germany, a Hay trying to apply the Golden Rule in international affairs, and a Sir Edward Grey endeavoring to restrain Europe from the brink of disaster. In all these cases, diplomatic methods are bound to respond to the demands and the policies of the statesmen at the head of the nation. Criticism, therefore, should be centred, not on Diplomacy in general, but on the policies which Diplomacy is instrumental in carrying into effect. The problem thus becomes a much larger one than the nature of Diplomacy: it concerns the formulation of national policies, and the ability of the crowd in the market-place to formulate these policies.

To grapple intelligently with this great problem, it is necessary, first of all, to be perfectly clear concerning the functions of Diplomacy in order to avoid certain common misapprehensions which render discussion of the whole subject difficult or impossible. Diplomacy has been well defined as "the art of negotiation." It is essentially the application to questions of an international nature, of the ordinary

The functions of Diplomacy

rules of negotiation among men, whether in law, business, politics, or any enterprise requiring relations with other men. It requires the same knowledge of men, the same keenness of insight, the same power of discussion, of persuasion; in sum, the same tact, or what we are accustomed to denote generally as common sense. It is true that there are special forms of etiquette, of technic in writing, and rules of the diplomatic game, which it is desirable to know; but they are not so obscure or complicated as many would infer. They are forms and rules which clever men master easily, and which are readily communicated by clerks and subordinate officials. Diplomacy is far from being what some would seem to suggest—a kind of "Sacred College" of Roman Fetiales, who have been initiated into the mysteries of diplomatic negotiation.

Success of untrained American Diplomats

The truth of this fact has been borne out in our own history since the days of Benjamin Franklin, our *first* Diplomat in every sense of the term. Franklin, Gallatin, Bancroft, Motley, Lowell, Adams, White, Choate, Reid, Herrick, the Pages, van Dyke, Gerard, and Morgenthau, are all instances of the ability of men chosen from public and private life to master the "Art of Negotiation." The qualities which made them successful as men of affairs at home were the very qualities essential for the duties of American Diplomats. To these qualities of mind, heart, and personality must be added the distinction of being, on the whole, truly representative Americans.

Granted, then, that Democracy can usually find able servants to protect its interests abroad, does it follow that Democracy is also able to direct their actions, and conduct its own foreign relations? Is Democracy competent to determine in the market-place—as Angell and others would insist—the great policies which its representatives are to execute? Must the President and his advisers hold Cabinet meetings in public, and take no action without first obtaining the approval of the populace?

Is Democracy competent for Diplomacy?

De Tocqueville in his great work on American Democracy remarks:

De Tocqueville's views

> As for myself, I do not hesitate to say that it is especially in the conduct of their foreign relations that Democracies appear to me decidedly inferior to other governments. . . . Democracy is favorable to the increase of the internal resources of a State; it diffuses wealth and comfort, promotes public spirit, and fortifies respect for law in all classes of society: all these are ad-

vantages which have only an indirect influence over the relations which one people bears to another. But a Democracy can only with great difficulty regulate the details of an important undertaking, persevere in a fixed design, and work out its execution in spite of serious obstacles. It cannot combine its measures with secrecy, or wait their consequences with patience.[1]

One may well differ from de Tocqueville in his preference for government by Aristocracy, but still find much force in his strictures regarding the incapacity of Democracy to carry on foreign relations. Our faith in the representative form of government in the United States may be fully justified, and yet we may well agree with de Tocqueville that there are great difficulties in the way of the "Democratization of Foreign Policies."

Need of secrecy in Diplomacy

A most important reason why Democracy is not fitted to conduct foreign relations is to be found in the need, alluded to by de Tocqueville, of secrecy, of at least a certain degree of secrecy, in diplomatic negotiations of a delicate nature, as, for example, the proposed purchase of the Danish West Indies by the United States. Those who urge publicity in foreign affairs can hardly hold that publicity in all human

[1] Chap. XIII.

affairs is possible or even desirable. It would not be maintained, for instance, that an industrial corporation could be successfully managed through public meetings of its board of directors and the disclosure to competitors of valuable information. The affairs of a university could not be carried on with due regard for the interests of all concerned by public meetings of the trustees or the faculty in the presence of the students and alumni. It is evident that there is hardly a human interest, whether of the family, private business, or public organization, where a certain degree of secrecy is not prudently required and eminently proper. There is nothing necessarily reprehensible in a wise reserve, a respect for privacy, a regard for sensibilities, a sincere concern for the adequate protection of legitimate interests.

How much truer this is in matters of international concern where vast interests must be properly safeguarded, and questions of extreme delicacy likely to embroil nations must be handled with consummate skill. If the President should have convincing evidence that a certain Power—Japan, for example—was intriguing against the United States and ready at any moment to take aggressive action, how much would it help in dealing with such a situation to make an official announcement of this fact? If the Administration were reliably informed that another Power was planning to get possession of the Danish West Indies for the purpose of establishing a naval base to menace American control of the Panama Canal, would it be prudent to so inform the American public and the world in general? Obviously, in either case, dangerous friction would be created, the diplomatic and military measures adopted by the Government to avert trouble would be largely nullified, and war very likely precipitated by such extraordinary disclosures.

<small>Value of publicity</small>

There is no doubt, of course, that a certain measure of publicity in affairs of state has been most effective at times in checking abuses and preventing corruption. It is clear, also, that the growth of constitutional government throughout the world, by its checks on Monarchy and Aristocracy, has been of great value in thwarting the evil designs, and in eliminating the dynastic wars of irresponsible monarchs. Publicity, the "thinking out loud" of Democracies, of which Lorimer speaks, has unquestionably served an excellent purpose. It is not necessary, however, to go to the extreme of saying that all affairs of state should be conducted with absolute publicity; that they are not subject to the ordinary rules of prudence, reserve, and secrecy observed in other human affairs. This would be quite unreasonable; and yet it is the kind of reasoning that vitiates the proposal for the "Democratization of Foreign Policies," the demand for public discussions in the market-place.

It should also be borne in mind that, by reason of their elevated position, their widened horizon, their comprehensive knowledge of international politics, their confidential avenues of information, the responsible statesmen of a nation are infinitely better fitted to deal intelligently with a trying diplomatic situation, a great crisis, than the people at large. In times of extreme tension created by such incidents as the sinking of the *Lusitania* and the *Sussex*, the general public, of course, is at once apprized of the main facts. The President, moreover, yielding to the importunate demands of the Press, is compelled to disclose just as much of the diplomatic negotiations as the exigencies of the situation and the best inter-

Comprehensive knowledge required in Diplomacy

ests of the country may permit. He cannot, however, take the public completely into his confidence. Even if he gives out the texts of important cipher messages before they are received by the other Government, he cannot with prudence or decency disclose the candid, though perhaps unauthorized, personal statements of the diplomatic representative of that Government in his loyal efforts to adjust the difficulty on an honorable basis. Partial information is thus worse than no information. The general public may reach entirely erroneous conclusions from the published correspondence, issued in part for "public consumption," when the most important features of the negotiations may have been treated in personal "conversations," which of necessity cannot be made a matter of record or publicly disclosed. Under such circumstances Democracy must either be discreetly patient or endanger the efforts of wise and patriotic statesmen to steer the Ship of State in time of storm.

American Democracy's attitude in foreign affairs

As a matter of practice, the American Democracy has usually shown remarkable restraint in times of international storm; has reposed great confidence in the President, and rallied in a non-partisan manner to his support. It has thereby confessed its own sense of incapacity to handle foreign affairs by any process of Initiative and Referendum. This was vividly demonstrated at the time of the occupation by American forces of the Mexican port of Vera Cruz in April, 1914. It was clear that few wanted war, or even intervention, and that many disapproved of the Administration's policy; and yet, the President had the loyal support of the whole country in the action he saw fit to take at that juncture. It will also be recalled how, at the time of the crisis with Germany over the sinking of the *Sussex*, when certain interests opposed to the policy of the President endeavored to curb his freedom by Congressional action, the whole country indignantly warned Congress to leave the control of foreign relations where it properly belongs, in the hands of the President and his advisers.

Other suggestive historical instances might be cited to advantage in this connection: Washington was compelled to face a most trying situation at the time of the French Revolution, when many Americans—Jefferson included—felt strongly convinced that the United States was bound by its Treaty of Alliance with

Washington's policy toward France

France to come to its aid against Great Britain. Washington, however, with as keen a sense of honor, but with a wider range of vision, a realization of all the factors involved, and an appreciation of the permanent best interests of the United States, wisely determined otherwise. As de Tocqueville justly observes, "nothing but the inflexible character of Washington, and the immense popularity which he enjoyed, could have prevented the Americans from declaring war against England. . . . The majority reprobated his policy, but it was afterward approved by the whole nation."[1]

Lincoln's policy in the "Trent" incident

Consider the situation confronting Lincoln at the time of the Mason-Slidell incident, when the North was exulting over the capture of the Confederate Commissioners from a British vessel, the *Trent;* and the British public, on the other hand, was aflame with indignation over what they considered a gross outrage. Only the patient, courageous, wise policy of Lincoln enabled the United States to reach a prudent and honorable settlement of the difficulty through diplomatic negotiation. It has been asserted with considerable show of reason, that if there had existed at that moment

[1] *Democracy in America*, chap. XIII.

DEMOCRACY AND DIPLOMACY 187

the same easy means of cable and wireless communication as at the present time, the same degree of publicity, war between England and the United States in all probability would have been inevitable. An inflamed public opinion in both countries would most likely have rendered a peaceful adjustment impossible.

Take the matter of the daring conspiracies on American soil by German official agents, as plainly proved in the cases of von Papen, Boy-Ed, and von Igel, all Attachés of the German Embassy in Washington. There is little doubt that if the Administration had disclosed to the American people all the mass of incriminating evidence in its possession, which was partially disclosed through British sources, public feeling would have run so high as to demand at least a complete rupture of diplomatic relations with Germany. Some may well believe that this would have been the only self-respecting course for the United States to take under the circumstances. The Administration evidently thought otherwise, and the American people, if they maintain their confidence in their representatives charged with so great responsibility, must believe that the best interests of the country were served by President Wilson's policy.

President Wilson's policy concerning German conspiracies

Democracy and Diplomacy

In all these three instances there is every reason to believe that discussion in the market-place and a direct, democratic control of foreign affairs would have resulted in very serious difficulties for the country. It would seem contrary to experience and reason to believe that Democracy would be any more able to avoid wars than would "Secret Diplomacy." Other instances, of course, might be profitably recalled to show the incapacity of Democracy to judge wisely, and act with calm, sure confidence in an international crisis, as, for example, the stupid intrusion of the French Chamber of Deputies in the policy of the Government, when England invited France to intervene jointly in Egypt. It would not seem necessary, however, to stress further this fundamental truth that Democracy is ill fitted to conduct foreign relations by market-place discussions. By way of résumé, this incapacity is due to three reasons: (1) the inability of the general public to be fully informed, to comprehend all the factors involved; (2) the supreme need of secrecy at certain moments in order to forward legitimate ends for the security of the State, and to avert trouble; and (3) what has been well characterized by de Tocqueville as the inability of Democracy to "regulate the details of an important undertaking, persevere in a fixed design, and work out its execution in spite of serious obstacles."

Except for those who never have sensed great responsibilities, who have only looked on from the "side lines," who have evolved in their armchairs splendid theories for the government of the State and the Universe, reasons of the character suggested would seem sufficient to indicate the folly of the proposition to encourage Democracy to take the control of international relations from the hands of its trusted statesmen. From the point of view of political theory the issue is to be drawn between those who believe in Direct Government—the restoration of a pure form of Athenian Democracy—and those who believe in truly Representative Government, which reposes confidence in and gives loyal support to those chosen to steer the Ship of State.

Issue between "Direct Government" and "Representative Government"

But it will be replied by some that, while the captain of a ship is responsible for navigation, the owners of the ship are entirely within their rights in determining the port of destination; that a whole people must be allowed to deter-

Inability of Democracy to determine policies

mine the policy of a nation, whether, for example, it be for war or peace. There would seem to be some truth in this argument, particularly if a people believe in non-resistance, or are gross materialists whose national motto is "anything for a quiet life," and who imagine that war may be avoided at all hazards. But a contemplation of history, of the mysterious, inexorable forces which seem to determine the destinies of nations; of the sudden storms that arise, the dangers, the tests of manhood, the appeals to honor and sense of duty—all tends to reveal the utter futility of attempting to formulate with any certainty a national policy able to confront any emergency. One is led to appreciate the profound truth of the epigram uttered by President McKinley: "Duty determines Destiny." And the ready, courageous recognition of national duty must necessarily lie with those charged with supreme responsibility, who are best able to judge of the exact situation, and the measures required for the security of the true interests of the State, and of international society in general.

Confidence of Democracy in its representatives

This, of course, exacts a high degree of trustfulness in its representatives on the part of Democracy, especially when one realizes the enormous power centred in the hands of the President as Commander-in-Chief of the Army and Navy, as well as of the forces of Diplomacy —his power to create, by the use or misuse of all these elements, a situation whereby the country may be plunged into war before Congress can exercise its prerogative of declaring war. If Democracy is ever betrayed by its representatives it can only withdraw its confidence and visit its scorn on them. This, it must be acknowledged, is a defect of any form of government other than pure Democracy. It would seem, however, in the light of previous considerations, an infinitely lesser defect than would be involved in requiring absolute publicity in foreign affairs, the consultation of the passengers by the captain of the ship at every emergency, the Initiative and Referendum, the "collective *un*wisdom" of the market-place.

The question naturally arises whether, if the people are not competent to direct and control Diplomacy, there is not therefore a necessity for diplomatic experts specially trained to represent the nation's interests abroad. It is quite common to assume as a matter of course that the United States should have a perma-

The Diplomatic Service

nent corps of trained Diplomats just as we have a permanent corps of experts in the Army and the Navy. Is this assumption correct? Is there a real analogy between the Diplomatic Service and the Army or the Navy?

No parallel between Diplomatic Service and Army or Navy

In the first place, it should be re-emphasized that the qualities necessary for success in Diplomacy are the very qualities necessary for pre-eminence and success in private and public life, namely, tact, knowledge of men, intelligence, courage, and, in general, what we are accustomed to call common sense. These are the possessions of no privileged class, whether of Diplomats or business men. They certainly are not the technical requirements which men in the Army and Navy must possess—that expert knowledge of guns and ships, machinery and organization, tactics and strategy. It is therefore most misleading to speak metaphorically of Diplomats as constituting the outer line of defense of a country, and hence requiring to be specially trained into a special corps as a co-ordinate Service with the Army and Navy. It is true that Diplomats occasionally require the aid of the Army and Navy, and that they often obviate the necessity for either, but it is not true that there is any real parallel between them as concerns expert knowledge and training.

A little reflection concerning certain facts, I am confident from personal experience, will lead one seriously to question the desirability of having a permanent, classified Diplomatic Service, offering, as the Army and Navy, a life career. One great objection lies in the accumulation of what a colleague in the British Diplomatic Service once characterized as "dead timber." A sure tenure of service, the attainment of a certain respectable rank, a substantial increase in one's family with all its increasing needs, a routine, bureaucratic method of transacting business, a perfunctory attitude toward matters of importance—all conduce most powerfully to a consequent lack of ambition, power of initiative, and a desire for quiet ease—to that condition characterized as "dead timber." Mere skill in the drafting of notes, in the orderly conduct of chancery work, in social address, can in no way compensate for the loss of that personal initiative, that keen interest and fresh enthusiasm which, as a rule, has distinguished most of the American Diplomatic representatives eager to make a credit-

Objections to permanent Diplomatic Service "dead timber"

able record during the uncertain time of their service abroad.

> "Representative" diplomats required

Another great objection to a permanent, classified Diplomatic Service is the danger to which diplomats are exposed, and—for some inexplicable reason—American diplomats in particular, of becoming denationalized to a certain extent, of becoming cosmopolitan to such a devitalizing degree that they may cease to be thoroughly representative of their country, in its varied interests, its national characteristics, its feelings, sympathies, and even its ideals. The prime requisite in a diplomat is that he should be absolutely representative, the faithful interpreter of his fellow countrymen, of their ideas, ideals, and highest interests. Anything which operates to deprive a man of direct, vital touch with the daily life, the swiftly changing life of a country like the United States, and with its intimate concerns, inevitably tends to render him less efficient as a diplomatic representative of his country.

> Freedom of President in choice of diplomats to execute policies

This fact is of special importance when it comes to the question of national policies. It is apparent that the United States has been unable to lay down the broad lines of permanent policies so that they may be automatically carried out and developed by successive Administrations. Even the Monroe Doctrine, which is generally regarded as a permanent policy, has been subjected to ever new and extraordinary interpretations that have profoundly altered its original character. Witness the "Receivership Policy" of President Roosevelt, the "Dollar Diplomacy" of President Taft, and the "Constitutionalism" of President Wilson. In all such instances the President, in the execution of his foreign policies, is fairly entitled to the services of men in direct touch and sympathy with the Administration and its purposes. He is entitled to the greatest freedom in selecting men of affairs, of large vision, and ability to properly represent the nation abroad. He cannot justly be circumscribed in his choice, whether for Panama, Pekin, or the Court of Saint James, to a list of men long in residence abroad and out of vital touch with their country, often without the peculiar qualifications required for appointment at a given moment to some post of special importance. He must be free to choose men of the stamp of Lowell, Hay, Herrick, van Dyke, Reinsch, and Francis.

Permanent Diplomatic Service undesirable

If the President be free—as he ought properly to be free—in his right of appointment—subject, of course, to the consent of the Senate—then all possibility of a permanent, classified Diplomatic Service is naturally eliminated. You cannot honestly hold out to a young man the prospect of a diplomatic career, if you cannot ensure his advancement above the rank of Secretary of Embassy, and when superannuated, the right of retirement under a pension. For the reasons before indicated, there can be no guarantee of a sure berth or an Embassy, except in case of conspicuous merit and unusual fitness for the particular post to be filled, as in the case of Mr. Fletcher, appointed Ambassador to Mexico.

Rich men not needed as diplomats

It may be objected that such a condition of affairs virtually means that only rich men can afford to represent their country abroad. This does not necessarily follow, however, though it is a fact that American diplomats have in many posts been notoriously underpaid. It is obviously incumbent on the Government to provide permanent Embassies and Legations, properly maintained as residences for its representatives, in order that they may worthily uphold the dignity of the country; and also compensate them sufficiently to enable them to render their services without personal sacrifice. It should be remarked, however, in passing, that it would undoubtedly be a misfortune if diplomatic posts were so well paid as to be an object for greedy politicians.

In regard to the positions of Secretaries of Embassies and Legations, which also should be well paid, if men of ambition are unwilling to risk their careers in so uncertain a service, then the United States must be content with such men as can be obtained. But, as a matter of fact, there are always to be found plenty of men of ability who, either because of independent means or the desire for foreign experience and special opportunities, are perfectly willing to take these lesser posts. It is true that some of them will be keenly disappointed because of a failure to secure promotion; but it cannot be charged that they have been misled into believing that they had been assured a permanent career, or eligibility for appointment whenever a vacancy should occur at London or Paris.

Secretaries of Embassies and Legations

The position taken here should not be interpreted as favoring the elimination of merit

Merit should be recognized

from the Diplomatic Service, or a plea for the "Spoils System." Exceptional merit should, of course, be rewarded where men have rendered diplomatic services of special value, and when their retention is essential for the best interests of the country. But even in such cases it rests necessarily with the President and the Secretary of State to determine who may have proved worthy of special recognition.

"Spoils System"

Nothing could be more reprehensible than the Bryan conception of finding well-paid jobs for "deserving Democrats." But where the President may desire to single out men of his own Party who are in sympathy with his policies and conspicuously fitted to represent the United States abroad, there is nothing inherently objectionable to his having the freedom to make such appointments.

Summary

By way of summary our considerations of the relation of Democracy to Diplomacy have led us to the three following general conclusions:

I. First of all, it is a fundamental error to confuse Diplomacy as a profession with the policies it may be called on to execute; to identify the agent with the principal; to centre criticism on the instrument rather than on the man who wields it. The methods of Diplomacy will depend primarily on the personalities of the statesmen responsible for the conduct of foreign affairs. The policy which may guide these statesmen and a nation as a whole may be good or bad, wise or imprudent, far-sighted or opportunistic, courageous or cowardly.

II. The determination of a nation's policy, whether in time of calm or of international storm, must rest largely in the hands of the responsible representatives chosen by Democracy to safeguard the nation's interests. The secrecy required to protect and forward national interests, the comprehensive knowledge of all the factors involved, the breadth of vision, the pertinacity of purpose, the sense of responsibility to future generations as well as to the present generation, all forbid the efficient management of a nation's vast interests by discussion in the market-place. The "Democratization of Foreign Policies" therefore cannot mean that Democracy, by a process of Initiative and Referendum, would commit the folly of refusing confidence and support to its responsible statesmen in times of diplomatic complications and international danger.

III. The large measure of freedom which

necessarily must be granted the President in his conduct of foreign relations must also logically include the greatest freedom in his choice of diplomatic agents for the execution of policies and the most effective representation of American interests. This means, of course, that a classified, permanent, Diplomatic Service—at least at the present stage of the country's development—is decidedly unwise and undesirable. Conspicuous merit should be recognized, and bad appointments vigorously condemned. The American people have the right and the obligation to insist on a high standard of Diplomacy and Diplomatic appointments. It still remains fundamentally true, however, that democracy, for its own good, must not attempt to embarrass the President and his advisers in their conduct of foreign affairs. It should frankly acknowledge—as it usually has been ready to acknowledge—in a loyal patriotic manner, its own inherent incapacity for Diplomacy.

CHAPTER X

THE SUBSTITUTION OF LAW FOR WAR

The horrors of modern warfare have driven many of its immediate victims insane. There is small excuse, however, for those who, far from the battle-field, have been so impressed by the terrible losses and suffering that they have lost the capacity to reason. Such persons can find no rational justification for war. They regard it as an anachronism, a reversion to savagery. In dealing with the great problems raised by the Great War, they are of as little service as would be a surgeon who should allow his mind to be diverted by the agony of the victim of cancer from the problem of its cure and its prevention. They seem incapable of analyzing the causes of war, or vaguely attribute it to Militarism, greed, and passion. It is enough that war is horrible; therefore it is without excuse.

The horror of war

Realizing the insufficiency of this kind of reasoning, some fall back on the false analogy that as men have abandoned duelling, so na-

Duelling and Arbitration; Self-Redress

tions should abandon war. Without understanding the limitations of Arbitration, they are convinced that it is an adequate substitute for the duel of war. We have seen how feeble and inadequate is Arbitration for the settlement of most of the disputes which are the efficient cause of war. As for duelling, a little reflection should convince one that modern warfare is not in any way like the duel; it is not a jousting match, a chivalric contest between plumed knights. Moreover, if by referring to the abolition of duelling one means that society no longer condones acts of self-redress, he is bound to show that international society has reached that advanced stage of development where self-redress is no longer necessary. Self-redress under the Common Law was not reprobated or forbidden, as in cases of the distraining of cattle, until the Law itself afforded adequate protection and remedy. It may well be questioned whether in certain instances of gross slander, or attacks on the person or the honor of a woman, modern society has really provided a satisfactory substitute for self-redress. One may well doubt whether the legal, peaceful method does not often savor of coarse materialism, and dull the finer sensibilities. However that may be, the history of any society—the Western Frontier of forty years ago, for example—will reveal that self-redress has every justification so long as society is unable to provide swift, satisfactory means of litigation, adequate punishment for wrong-doing, and the effective prevention of nuisance, disorder, and crime. In the West, hanging for horse stealing and drastic measures of retribution for wrong-doing formerly had the moral approbation of such public opinion as then existed. So, likewise, with international society; it has by no means reached that stage of development where it can with safety dispense with the right of self-redress. The evolution of an adequate system of law to administer international justice, the establishment of courts empowered to interpret such law, and the creation of the means of its enforcement without endangering the rights of States, all this remains yet to be accomplished before the right of international self-redress can reasonably be abolished.

A fundamental error in the reasoning of peace extremists who so confidently urge disarmament, the abolition of international "duels," the substitution of Arbitration for

What is peace?

war, and the establishment of "leagues to enforce peace," would seem to lie in a failure to understand the very nature of peace itself. They would appear to regard peace as something to be *willed*, to be had if men only desire it. They speak of it as something tangible, to be sought after, overtaken, and captured. No elaborate argument is required to show that peace is essentially a *state*, a result. Like virtue or contentment, it comes with honorable conduct, with righteous behavior. Like pleasure, "it is only a by-product." Peace cannot be divorced from righteousness. It is to be had only when men rectify wrong, punish evil-doers, and guarantee justice to all. There is a "divine discontent" which can never tolerate with self-respect a "peaceful" condition of affairs based on cruelty and injustice.

The horrors of peace

We need again to remind ourselves of conditions within our own borders where strikes, and civil warfare even, have lasted for weeks and months, as in Colorado and West Virginia. Where society has been negligent or unwilling to provide adequate agencies for the investigation of the rights and wrongs of Labor and Capital, it should not lift its hands in holy horror if violence occurs, and peace is not to be had. We are bound to recognize that industrial conditions may exist where the struggle for mere existence is painful; where life becomes a burden; where crime and vice abound; and where peace is a hideous mockery. There is bodily suffering and mental anguish that far exceed the sufferings and anguish of warfare. There are horrors of peace as well as of war. All this we are constrained to acknowledge, and seek, as far as we are able, to eradicate the wrongs, the cruelties, and the injustice that often render peace impossible and, at times, even undesirable.

The catastrophe which has overwhelmed Europe has also overwhelmed thinking men the world over. It is entirely inexplicable to many. It seems to threaten the very foundations of International Law, and to forever discredit Christianity itself. The situation is unquestionably discouraging; but it is not the irrational situation many would have it appear. Men of finite intelligence cannot accurately measure all the factors that influence the destinies either of individuals or nations. They may learn from practical experience and from history, however, that there is a reason behind

The European catastrophe

all phenomena, whether of nature, or society. We know that scientific methods of investigation will generally reveal the immediate or primary cause behind every effect.

It is in this dispassionate, scientific manner that we should approach the investigation of international phenomena. In the midst of historical obscurity, of diplomatic chicanery, of the din of battles, and the heat of passion, we are able to discern some of the causes that lead men to substitute war for law. Just as the physician ignores external symptoms and goes direct to the physical causes of disease, so, also, the international diagnostician is not misled by the external manifestations of the ills of nations. He knows full well that whatever men may think, say, or do, controversies between nations which often lead to war usually have a definite, deep-seated cause. They are not artificial, the product of an excited imagination. He knows that the body politic has its ills as well as the human body. He knows that what is often most needed is not psychic treatment or exorcism, but drastic measures, sometimes involving the shedding of blood.

European catastrophe explicable

To the scientific student of international affairs, therefore, it is not at all inexplicable that Europe should now be racked with a consuming fever, agonizing pains, and sufferings almost beyond the power of endurance. The wonder is that Europe has not sooner succumbed to the diseases preying on its vitals. A failure to live sanely in obedience to sound principles of health must inevitably entail sickness and death. It is because the statesmen of Europe have repeatedly ignored and affronted the sound principles of international health that their nations now find themselves brought so low.

Charles Dupuis, in his remarkable book, *L'Équilibre Européen*, makes the following vigorous statement:

Balance of Power

The experience of three centuries has demonstrated that, far from insuring respect for the rights of all, the principle of the Balance of Power resulted merely in causing the powerful States to concede that every acquisition of territory made by one of them might justify equivalent acquisitions on the part of the rest. . . . Powerless to introduce peace and justice into international relations, it has veiled with specious and virtuous pretexts unjust ambitions, baleful wars, and veritable operations of brigandage.[1]

And Lawrence, in *Principles of International Law*, also adds his severe word of indictment

[1] P. 96.

of the vicious "principle" which has heretofore governed the counsels of Europe:

> It takes no account of any other motives of state policy than the personal aggrandizement of rulers and the territorial extension of States. It distributes provinces and rounds off the boundaries of kingdoms without regard to the wishes of the populations and their affinities of race, religion, and sentiment.[1]

These denunciations are probably too sweeping in character, as restrictive measures, and fresh groupings of nations may at times have been a necessity to self-protection against certain aggressive and unprincipled nations. It would seem clear, however, that the mischievous and lamentable results of the Congresses of Vienna and Berlin should have been a sufficient warning to Europe. It is incredible that scheming diplomats should have parcelled out immense territories as a grocer cutting cheese, and apportioned the populations of the different countries as cattle drivers at a market. And yet this vicious idea is again at work. Men to-day are pointing out the danger of permitting Russia to expand farther. They are pleading the necessity of dividing Germany as a safeguard for the peace of Europe! Accord-

[1] *Principles of International Law*, 3d ed., p. 129.

ing to this pernicious doctrine, if the population of a given State should outstrip the population of a neighboring State, or if one should become vastly more wealthy than the other, there must then be a new readjustment of territory to re-establish a balance!

Such reasoning is preposterous. There never can be among nations, any more than in the physical world, or in human affairs, a stable equilibrium of forces. Nothing is permanent in international affairs; but there is no reason why nations should not honestly try to do justice to each other's legitimate interests. There is no reason why they should not obey sound principles when confronted with the solemn responsibility of tracing anew the boundaries of Europe. The maintenance of a "balance of power" has proved as futile as it has proved vicious. It would now seem high time to abandon the pursuit of this *ignis fatuus*.

Futility of Balance of Power

If it be contended that Europe cannot tolerate the menace of Pan-Germanism, or Pan-Slavism, the answer that history repeats in melancholy tones is, that it is more dangerous to thwart nationalistic aspirations than to permit their natural, normal realization. Europe

Rights of nationalities

has less to fear from the recognition of the legitimate desires of outraged nationalities than from the cynical denial of such claims. There can be no true peace nor any justification for peace that is not based on the sound, righteous principle of respect for the legitimate claims and interests of every nation, whether conquered or victorious, small or great. The Great War will have been largely in vain if the nations concerned invoke again the iniquitous principle of the Balance of Power when they assemble to remake the map of Europe.

Sound principles

If the principle of the Balance of Power has failed hitherto to insure peace, what, then, are the principles which should be applied in laying the foundations of peace and of the law which must regulate the peaceful relations of States?

Community of interests

I. First of all there is the basic principle of "community of interests," that "body of convictions" which justifies the existence of separate, autonomous nations. I have endeavored to suggest in the chapter on Nationalism the various factors which must be taken into account in determining this community of interests. We have seen that they may be roughly classified as: (1) pyschological, according to racial or temperamental preferences and prejudices; (2) political, according to instinctive preferences for different political institutions; (3) economic, according to the peculiar needs of various peoples; and (4) ethical, as concerning the national pursuit of ideals. It is evident that all these factors must be duly weighed and respected in any attempt to reconstruct the map of Europe. It is not easy, of course, to determine with any precision the community of interests that leads men to prefer one nation to another. The factors mentioned are not only difficult to measure, but are even at times antagonistic. An instance of this is found in Trieste, where Italian nationalistic interests and Austrian economic interests are in conflict. The reconciliation of such conflicting interests in some just compromise as the establishment of a "free port," for example, demands the highest statesmanship. The generous, tolerant spirit of mutual respect, however, of "give and take," should never render even such situations incapable of a fair solution.

The wishes of the peoples immediately concerned must, of course, be given first consideration in any alteration of boundaries. The principle of a plebiscite to ascertain their

Plebiscites

preferences is unmistakably just though not always possible of application. Germany at first recognized this in respect to Northern Schleswig and subsequently repudiated her pledge. The inhabitants of the Danish West Indies have a right to be consulted before the Islands are made the subject of barter. If a certain territory offers peculiar economic or strategic advantage to a given nation, however, the inhabitants of such territory must not be permitted in a spirit of narrow provincialism to decide the larger questions at issue. The right of the people on the coast, for example, to prevent the cession or the free use of a port to the people of the *hinterland* should obviously be given but slight consideration. In a similar way, Colombia was entitled to little sympathy in its pretensions to stand in the way of the establishment of interoceanic communication across the international highway of Panama by the nation most vitally concerned and best able to accomplish the task.

Conflicts of interests

There will inevitably arise serious conflicts of interests and great issues concerning such strategic points as Panama, Gibraltar, Constantinople, and elsewhere. It will be difficult in many instances to determine with justice the exact nature and relative value of national community of interests. Whatever the difficulties may be, it would seem clear that the principle of the recognition of national community of interests should be the solid basis of all attempts to recast the boundaries of nations. As a sound, scientific principle for the foundation of peace and International Law it can safely challenge the cynical, disastrous principle of the Balance of Power.

II. The second great principle which should be observed in many instances, is that of Autonomy, the granting of the right of complete local self-government. There may be insuperable difficulties in the way of conceding fully the claims of the Poles, Bohemians, Hungarians, Armenians, and others to independent national existence. Association, union, and any form of forcible inclusion with other peoples may be most repugnant. It may be made endurable, however, by the application of the principle of Autonomy. This principle would probably afford a fairly adequate solution of nationalistic problems in most instances, even in the case of Alsace-Lorraine. Furthermore, we should bear in mind the fact that a State like Canada, though remaining an inte-

Principle of Autonomy

gral portion of the Empire, might yet enjoy a separate, autonomous status entitling it to some form of international recognition. The very least concession which prudence and justice exact is the granting of the just claims of men of all races and nationalities to a full measure of self-government. In the recognition of this principle lies one of the chief guarantees of enduring peace.

Principle of Freedom of Trade

III. The third great principle which should be respected in the reconstruction of boundaries is that of International Freedom of Trade. There are natural reasons, as we have seen, why men should prefer the maintenance of national frontiers. The creation of tariff frontiers, however, leads to artificial differences and international controversies which are hard to justify. A tariff war, in its pressure and powers of economic strangulation, as in the case of Serbia at the hands of Austria, though not spectacular is quite as real as actual warfare. The announced intention of the Entente Allies, therefore, to concert measures of economic defense against the Teutonic Powers, after the Great War, is merely another way of continuing the war. It thus constitutes a grave men-

SUBSTITUTION OF LAW FOR WAR 215

ace to the re-establishment of the peace of Europe. It cannot be too severely condemned.

While it is plainly the interest of each nation to make itself as self-supporting and self-sufficient as possible, nations are bound to be economically interdependent in many respects. Freedom of exchange in certain products is almost a vital necessity. They may achieve a certain degree of independence by erecting legislative, protective boundaries, but they do so only at the cost of bitter antagonisms. History shows how lamentable and futile have been the Chauvinistic attempts of such nations as Spain and England to maintain an exclusive control of the trade of colonies, for example. Economic weapons in such instances are merely substituted for the cruder weapons of international warfare. *Economic interdependence*

The importance of this principle of International Freedom of Trade is to be seen in connection with such an abnormal situation as Trieste. Whether that Port should belong to Italy or Austria would not very much matter, provided it remained a "free port." So, likewise, with Serbia: if access to the Adriatic through the actual possession of a port like *"Commercial Access"*

216 *INTERNATIONAL REALITIES*

Durazzo should not prove feasible, the guarantee at least of the "commercial freedom of access," formerly suggested by the Powers, would be eminently just.

Wide application of principle

It will be seen that the extension of this economic principle, either through the removal of tariff frontiers or the creation of "free ports," is of the greatest importance for international peace. One of its chief virtues is its applicability to widely divergent situations. If the Poles, for example, could not properly lay claim, at this late day, to a complete national restoration, perfect freedom of trade with their neighbors would do much to reconcile them to their qualified international status. Should it prove possible, on the other hand, to recognize the right of a people to a separate, national existence—the Serbs or the Hungarians, for example—perfect freedom of trade would doubtless be necessary to enable them effectively to maintain their political independence.

Three principles mutually complementary

It is interesting to note, by way of summary, how fully these three fundamental principles complement each other. The recognition of Community of Interests is of primary importance, and logically implies political independence. The recognition, however, of the principle of Autonomy, the right of local self-government, may make it possible to recognize a national community of interests without conceding full political independence in the sense generally laid down by writers on International Law. In any event, the recognition of the principle of International Freedom of Trade will go far toward enabling these organized States, whether independent or autonomous, to work out successfully their special problems, and live in harmony with their neighbors.

If the Great Powers undertake the momentous task of recasting the map of Europe in a spirit of revenge, of passion-blinded adherence to the utterly vicious principle of the Balance of Power, they will only have sown the seeds of future wars. The fearful conflict will have been in vain. If they are prepared, however, to face their sacred responsibilities with the earnest desire "to deal justly" with each other in obedience to generous, sound, scientific principles, this ghastly war, in its rectification of centuries of wrong, will have proved an incalculable blessing to the world.

Terms of peace

Rights and obligations

Assuming that the nations of the world are now prepared to lay the solid foundations of permanent peace and of a scientific system of International Law, we still encounter other difficulties of a serious character. The first requisite for political association is a common conception of rights and obligations. There can be no satisfactory system of law, no courts, no enforcement of law on any other basis. This truth is often forgotten when we speak of bringing about some form of international organization. There is an unfortunate tendency to argue that the causes of international friction and antagonisms will be removed at once by nations merely "getting together." The necessity of common ideas of right and wrong, of identic ideals of justice, as well as of a common abhorrence of war, is not at all clearly recognized.

Divergent views of nations

Whatever the right or wrong of the Great War, it is lamentably clear that there exists a most serious divergence of views between the opposing nations in respect to the rights and obligations of States. The Prussian valuation of treaties, for example, is of such a nature as to constitute a grave menace to the peace of the whole world. International rela-

SUBSTITUTION OF LAW FOR WAR 219

tions cannot peacefully be maintained without a due regard for treaty engagements, and particularly for the rights of weaker and smaller nations. The only other alternative is a perpetual state of war, whether of actual combat, or the terrific strain of armaments. International Law cannot be built on foundations laid in accordance with the Prussian theory of rights and obligations. Before we can have a normal, logical evolution of the law of nations, we must be agreed on its basic principles. Germany and the United States, Italy and Japan, Russia and China, Brazil and France—all the nations of the world—must first think fundamentally alike before they can trust each other, "pool their interests," and unite firmly within an international system of law.

To state this fact is to suggest the enormity of the task. General education and the cultivation of closer intimacies and interests can alone bring nations to think alike. It will probably require a very long time for nations to learn to trust each other within a common organization capable of legislating wisely concerning vital interests of mutual concern. The administration of justice between them can—

Need of mutual understanding

not be had until they are agreed on fundamental principles of law. The people of the United States, sharing fairly similar notions of justice and possessing a model Constitution, were unable to avoid the Civil War. Let us therefore not be so foolish as to believe that the diverse nations of the world have yet reached that stage of development and capacity for political organization where justice can be effectively administered and law be substituted for war.

Status of International Law

When we appreciate fully the significance of this fact of the utter lack of a common conception of rights and obligations between nations, we find nothing extraordinary in recognizing that International Law is still in a rudimentary stage of development. It is true, of course, that the courts of most nations, arbitral tribunals—to a lesser extent—and diplomatic negotiations, constantly acknowledge a large body of usage and agreements which have become incorporated in International Law. They moreover concede it the full status of *law*, the followers of Austin to the contrary, notwithstanding. There is but a very small portion of the law of nations, however, which may be called positive law in the same sense as municipal statute law. When one considers the vast field of interests involved in international relations, he realizes how pitifully small is the body of law which may be said to have received the positive assent of nations. Take, for example, the single important question of the rights of foreign creditors. Leading as it often does to inordinate demands, and even to a loss of national independence, this question is one of the most dangerous that can arise between nations. There is no law whatever, no understanding, even, by which the rights of foreign creditors may be ascertained, and the proper procedure for the prosecution of their rights prescribed. (The Hague Convention of 1907 concerning the Recovery of Contract Debts, which justifies the use of force to collect debts, and which has failed of general acceptance, is entitled to but slight consideration.) Or take the great field of international torts where aliens have been wronged by acts of the State or of its officials. Here again we have one of the most fruitful causes of controversy and conflict; and yet International Law is practically dumb on the whole subject. Consider that neglected and supremely important portion of the law of nations fitly en-

Rights of foreign creditors

International torts

Conflict of Laws

titled: "Conflict of Laws," where delicate questions constantly arise concerning rights of national jurisdiction and the law to be applied. Nothing could be more unreasonable or unjust than to relegate matters of guardianship, inheritance, and even of domicile and nationality, to the limbo of "Conflict of Laws." They are peculiarly the very questions which should most concern the law of nations. It surely has no *raison d'être* if it cannot regulate the rights of individuals as travellers or sojourners throughout the world. These are rights which should inhere in a person, not as a Britisher or a German, but as a *citizen of the world*. This whole field, however, is practically undeveloped. Some of the European nations have endeavored by special agreements to bring order out of chaos; but "Conflict of Laws" still remains a constant accusation against International Law. And perhaps the greatest obstacle in the way of regulating this portion of the law of nations is the Anglo-American school of jurisprudence which holds provincially to the theory of the exclusive jurisdiction of the territorial sovereign, and to the supremacy of Common Law. Nothing could more clearly suggest the chaos reigning in this field of International Law than the very situation within the borders of the United States, where the laws of forty-eight different States are in conflict.

I have not taken into consideration, in this discussion, the law of war, because of the fact that it is, in final analysis, the very negation of law itself. International Law cannot concern itself with the suspension of law. Its mission is to regulate the *peaceful* relations of States. Our whole purpose has been to consider the law of nations as a substitute for war.

International Law and war

As a general result of our endeavors to understand the great fundamental realities of international life, I think it should be apparent that the creation of law as an adequate substitute for war is a laborious undertaking that calls for great patience, courage, wisdom, and faith. Its coherent, natural growth cannot be unduly accelerated. Nations may do much, however, to crystallize into formal agreements many principles of law already accepted in part in actual usage. Societies of International Law may help materially by their discussions and propaganda to educate international public opinion. Nations may thus come to a com-

Creation of International Law

mon understanding on many questions of vital importance concerning the rights and obligations of States. Working along different, converging lines, they may thus come ultimately to the same goal—the realization of essentially common conceptions of international justice.

International conferences

International conferences, such as gathered at The Hague in 1899 and 1907, might do much to facilitate the creation of International Law. The Hague Conferences, however, suffered most unfortunately from two obsessions. Preoccupied with thoughts of the coming Great War, they devoted their energies principally to the drafting of futile regulations to govern the conduct of war. They also attempted to create courts of "arbitral justice" before there was any agreement concerning the nature of "justiciable" questions, or the law to be applied by these courts. The notable failure of the Hague Conferences to direct their energies along the constructive lines of creating International Law to govern the *peaceful* relations of States is deeply to be deplored. This is the real and the arduous task which must be undertaken; not fervid crusades to induce nations to disarm and arbitrate. War is a grewsome—and it may be at times an irrational—method

SUBSTITUTION OF LAW FOR WAR 225

of settling disputes. But until we can demonstrate that a thoroughly effective, rational substitute for war has been devised, nothing could be more irrational than to ask nations "to turn their swords into ploughshares."

Human progress is exasperatingly slow. It requires many generations to gain any considerable victories for civilization. And even then, strenuous battles must be fought to hold the ground already won. The man who would make his effective contribution to the great cause of international good relations must abandon abstractions and illusions. Though holding to his ideals, he must ask to have his eyes opened to a vision of things as they are, as well as to a vision of things as they should be. The greatest generals, scientists, statesmen, and reformers have been those who, full of vision and faith, dealt with and overcame brute obstacles and crude facts. It is this type of man the world most needs at the present time in dealing with the great international realities that now confront us.

International progress

In conclusion, I venture again to reiterate that "our task, therefore, as defenders and upbuilders of International Law, becomes one

The task

of determining the specific mutual interests which nations are prepared to recognize; and then to endeavor, in a spirit of toleration, friendly concern, and scientific open-mindedness, to formulate the legal rights and obligations which these interests entail. Having come to a substantial agreement concerning the law itself, we may then properly turn to the task of securing the most effective agencies for its interpretation and enforcement. The nations of the earth are far from ready to be ruled by a common, sovereign, political authority. Their interests and ways of thinking are still too antagonistic for that. The great preliminary work of facilitating closer relations, of removing misunderstandings, of reconciling conflicting points of view, of identifying various interests, of fostering common conceptions of rights and obligations, remains yet to be done." The substitution of law for war is a stupendous task. It is therefore a most inspiring task.

INDEX

Agadir, 92.
Alabama Arbitration (see Geneva Arbitration).
Alaska, 38, 39.
Albania, 83.
American Continent (see Pan-Americanism):
 special problems of, 148.
 duty of U. S. toward, 148.
 organization of American nations, 170.
American Institute of International Law, 56, 68.
American Society of International Law, 162.
Anarchism, 41.
Andorra, 35.
Angell, Norman, 150, 155, 175.
Arbitration:
 and International Law, 19.
 limitations of, 75, 158.
 ignorance of, 75.
 Pious Funds, 87.
 Venezuelan Preferential Claims, 88.
 Japanese House Tax, 88.
 Mascat Dhows, 88.
 Maritime Boundary (Norway and Sweden), 88.
 Canevaro Claim, 88.
 Russian Indemnity, 88.
 Casablanca, 89.
 Savarkar, 89.
 Carthage and *Manouba*, 89.
 North Atlantic Fisheries, 90.
 Dogger Bank incident, 91.
 unsuited for political questions, 93.
 suited for unimportant matters, 94.
 not justice, 95.
 a triumph for Diplomacy, 97, 145.
 not understood by pacifists, 144.
 not for punitive purposes, 145.
 propaganda embarrassing to Europe, 146.
 as a substitute for war, 202.

Armed Neutralities, 128.
Australia, 63.
Austria-Hungary, 27, 29, 84, 122, 214, 215.
Autonomy:
 value of principle of, 213, 217.

Bahamas, 39.
"Balance of Power," 32, 82, 165, 207, 209, 217.
Balkan War, 32, 82.
Bavaria, 63, 66.
Belgium, 13, 152.
Belligerents:
 conflict of interests of neutrals with interests of, 5.
Bermudas, 39.
Bernstorff, Count von, 121.
Blaine, 159.
Bluntschli, 45.
Boers, 79.
Bonfils, 72.
Boundaries, 40.
Bucharest, Treaty of, 83.
Bulgaria, 49, 83.

Canada, 14, 63, 66, 213.
Canevaro Claim Arbitration, 88.
Carthage and *Manouba* Arbitration, 89.
Casablanca Arbitration, 89.
Cattaro, 38.
Central America, 171.
China, 80.
Colombia, 29, 212.
Colonial Empire:
 problem of, 81.
"Commercial Access," 215.
Commission of American Jurists, 168.
Community of Interests:
 factors constituting, 24.
 language, 24.
 religion, 25.
 political sympathies, 25.
 customs, traditions, 26.
 economic factor, 27.
 revenues, 27.

INDEX

geographical factor, 27.
external pressure, 29.
basis of Nationalism, 34, 54, 210.
conflicts of interests, 212.
Principle of, 213, 216.
Confederacy, the Southern, 120.
Conflict of Laws (see International Private Law).
Congress of Berlin, 32, 59, 82, 146, 208.
Congress of Vienna, 14, 59, 146, 208.
Constantinople, 28, 40, 110, 212.
Contract Debts:
 convention concerning recovery of, 3.
 need of law concerning, 147, 221.
Court of Arbitral Justice, 96.
Cuba, 13, 52, 65.
Customs, Traditions, 26.
Czar of Russia, 158.

Danish West Indies, 180, 182, 212.
Danube Commission, 109.
Democracy:
 international value of, 44.
 and Diplomacy, 174, 179, 188, 198.
 views of de Tocqueville concerning conduct of foreign relations by, 179.
 value of publicity in, 182.
 importance of executive direction of foreign affairs in, 183.
 attitude of American democracy toward foreign affairs, 184.
 incapacity for Diplomacy, 189.
Denmark, 27.
Despotism, 41.
De Tocqueville, 179, 186.
Dette Publique, 111.
Dickinson, G. Lowes, 175.
Diplomacy:
 and International Law, 19.
 Arbitration a triumph for, 97, 145.
 Democracy and, 174, 179, 188, 198.
 misapprehension of functions of, 175.
 merely an agent, 176.
 functions of, 177.
 success of American Diplomats, 178.

need of secrecy in, 180.
comprehensive knowledge required, 183.
attitude of American democracy toward foreign affairs, 184.
democracy incapable of, 189.
the Diplomatic Service, 191, 196.
Diplomats should be representative, 194.
freedom of President in choosing diplomats, 194.
permanent Diplomatic Service undesirable, 196.
Secretaries of Embassies and Legations, 197.
"Spoils System," 198.
Diplomatic Settlements:
 concerning Samoa, 91.
 Anglo-French agreement of 1904, 92.
 Anglo-Russian agreement of 1907, 92.
 Moroccan agreement, 92.
Dogger Bank Incident, 91.
Dollar Diplomacy, 160.
Duelling, 201.
Dupuis, Charles, 207.

Economic Factor, 27, 215.
Economic Warfare, 37, 214.
Egypt, 51, 65, 92, 188.
England (see Great Britain).
Enlistments, 124.
Equality, 13:
 of States, 15.
 human inequalities, 67.
 of nations, 68.
 corollary of right to exist, 69.
 based on law of nature, 70.
 inequalities of nations, 70.
 theory opposed to international organization, 71.
 theory unsound, 72.
 definition of, 72.
Ethics, 31, 49.
Ethnology:
 ethnic and ethical ideals, 31.
European Problems:
 distinct from American, 146.
Existence:
 of States, 14, 58.
 "right" to, 14, 164.

INDEX

Nationalism basis of right to, 60.
  legal right to, 60.
Exterritoriality, 112.

Finland, 28.
France, 51, 92, 153, 185, 188.
Franco-Prussian War, 121, 130, 146.
Freedom of Trade, 214, 216.

Gareis, Karl:
  definition of law, 10.
  definition of International Law, 11.
  views on sanction of International Law, 20, 104.
Geneva Arbitration, 95, 97, 120, 130.
Germany, 20, 43, 86, 91, 121, 154, 187, 208, 212, 218.
Golden Rule:
  basis of International Law, 21, 104.
Great Britain, 28, 51, 91, 92, 120, 121, 128, 144, 153, 188, 215.
Greece, 49.
Grey, Sir Edward, 153, 177.
Grotius, 7, 130.
Gypsies, 36.

Hague Arbitration Tribunals, 19.
Hague Conventions:
  Rights and Duties of Neutral Powers, 131.
  The Pacific Settlement of International Disputes, 147.
  Recovery of Contract Debts, 147, 221.
Hague Peace Conferences, 2, 71, 145, 147, 158, 224.
Haldane, Lord, 154.
Heligoland, 39.
"Hinterland" Doctrine, 38, 39, 212.
Holland, 27.

Independence:
  nature of "right," 61.
  nations not truly independent, 62.
  not essential for recognition, 62.
  "right" of, an assumption, 63.
  "right," the claim to freedom, 64.

  synonymous with sovereignty, 65.
Interests:
  of States, 56, 58.
International Administration, 99:
  existing agencies for, 109.
    Danube Commission, 109.
    Suez Canal, 109.
    Tangiers, 109.
    Spitzbergen, 109.
    Constantinople, 110.
    Sanitary Board, 111.
    Dette Publique, 111.
    exterritoriality, 112.
    international unions, 112.
    Pan-American Union, 114.
International Bankruptcy, 148.
International "Clearing House," 114.
International Community, 102.
International Conferences and Congresses, 104.
International Creditors, 148, 221.
International Executive, 52, 106.
International High Commission on Uniformity of Laws, 169.
International Law:
  how discredited, 1.
  relation to war, 3.
  rights of neutrals under, 4.
  true function of, is to avert war, 6, 223.
  unscientific in method, 7.
  wrongly identified with natural law, 7.
  definition of, 11.
  failure of, to define rights of States, 13.
  fundamental problem of, 16.
  value of, 18.
  Diplomacy and, 19.
  Arbitration and, 19.
  and Municipal Law, 19.
  true sanction of, 20.
  true task of, 21.
  Golden Rule the basis of, 21, 104.
  nationalism and, 30, 34.
  not based on abstractions, 57, 74.
  universal in application, 61.
  unlike municipal law, 103.
  administered by national courts, 106.

INDEX

is truly law, 107.
definition of rights required, 107.
conflict of laws, 107.
Monroe Doctrine a part of, 164.
the creation of, 166, 223.
rights and obligations under, 218.
in a rudimentary stage of development, 220.
reconstruction of, 225.

International Legislation:
need of, 148, 166.
rights of foreign creditors, 148, 221.
bankruptcy, 148.
torts, 148.
rights of aliens, 148.
conferences for, 224.

International Private Law, 148, 166, 222.
International Prize Court, 71.
International Torts, 107, 148, 221.
International Tribunal, 105.
Internationalism, 33, 103.
Ireland, 25, 28.
Italy, 81, 215.

Japan:
California question, 43.
War with Russia, 79.
House Tax Arbitration, 88.
Dogger Bank incident, 91.
Relations with U. S., 181.
Jews, 35, 36.
"Justiciable":
meaning of term, 96, 224.

Kant, 100.
Korea, 80.
"Kultur":
defined as Nationalism, 30.

Lansing, Secretary, 122.
Law:
nature of, 9.
purpose and definition of, 10.
problem of, 11.
enforcement of, 17.
substitution of law for war, 173, 201.
abandonment of duelling and self-redress, 201.

Law of Nature (Natural Law):
falsely identified with International Law, 7.
true significance of, 9.
fallacies of, 11.
and theory of equality, 70.
Lawrence, T. J., 207.
League to Enforce Peace, 106, 137.
Loans, 125.
London Naval Conference, 70.
Lorimer, James, 21, 31, 41, 44, 53, 64, 99, 101, 127, 131, 135, 152.

Maritime Boundary Arbitration (Sweden and Norway), 88.
Mascat Dhows Arbitration, 88.
Mason and Slidell (Case of the *Trent*), 186.
Mexico, 87, 160, 185.
Militarism:
as a cause of war, 140.
meaning of, 141.
Monroe Doctrine:
disquieting extensions and interpretations of, 161, 195.
as interpreted by Mr. Root, 162.
as a sanction of International Law, 164.
regarded as Pan-American doctrine, 162, 165.
as a permanent policy, 195.
Montenegro, 38, 84.
Moral Personality of States, 53.
Morocco, 13, 14, 51, 58, 92, 94, 164.
Municipal Law, 19, 103.
Munitions:
embargo on, 120, 130.
complaint of U. S. against Great Britain, 120.
complaint of Germany against U. S., 121.
complaint of Germany against Great Britain, 121.
impossibility of defining, 124.

Nationalism:
rights of nationalities, 16, 105, 209.
nature of, 23.
community of interests, basis of, 24, 54.
and "Kultur," 30.
statesmen and idealists enemies of, 32.

INDEX

not opposed to internationalism, 33.
basis of international law, 34.
basis of right to exist, 60.
opposed by Pacifism, 151.
necessity for, 153.

Nations:
interdependence of, 36, 215.
controlling forces of, 47.
vital interests and honor of, 51, 52.
no common judge of, 52.
no absolute right to exist, 59.
not truly independent, 62.
equality of, 68.
inequalities of, 70.
divergent views of, 86, 218.
distinction between individual and, 101.
definition of interests of, 104.
no coercion possible, 105.
family of, 133, 134.

Neutrality:
nature of, 123.
sale of ships and arms by neutrals, 123.
enlistments, 124.
loans, 125.
not "a continuance of a state of peace," 126.
an abnormal state, 127.
"benevolent" neutrality, 130.
difficulties of, 131.
not indifference, 136.

Neutralization, 40.

Neutrals:
rights of, 4, 128.
disabilities of, 5.
conflict of interests with belligerent interests, 5, 125, 127.
obligations of, 129.
cannot adapt attitude to changing fortunes of war, 130.
true interests of, 133.
duty of intervention by, 134.
Hague Convention of 1907 concerning duties of, 147.

North Atlantic Fisheries Arbitration, 90.

Norway, 27.

Ottoman Empire, 25, 58, 81, 93.

Pacifism:
dangers of, 140, 156.
meaning of, 141.
expects too much of International Law, 143, 145.
arbitration propaganda embarrassing to Europe, 146.
the true task of, 147.
duty of Pacifists toward American problems, 149.
fosters cowardice and materialism, 150.
ignores spiritual values, 150.
opposed to Nationalism, 151.
a contributing cause of war, 153.
opposed to preparedness, 155.

Panama, 13, 28, 40, 51, 62, 65, 182, 212.

Pan-Americanism, 158:
purpose of, 159.
mistakes of, 160.
Monroe Doctrine as a Pan-American doctrine, 162, 165.
Commission of Jurists, 168.
International High Commission on Uniformity of Laws, 169.
First Pan-American Financial Conference, 169.
organization of American nations, 170.

Pan-American Union, 114:
possible utility of, 115, 170.
development of, 149.
purpose of, 159.

Peace:
nature of, 203.
horrors of, 204.
substitution of law for war, 173, 201, 223.

Persia, 13, 14, 51, 58, 92, 94.
Pious Funds Arbitration, 87.
Ports, Rivers, 37, 39, 211.
Preparedness, Military, 155.

President Wilson:
and Pan-Americanism, 160.
and German conspiracies, 187.
"constitutionalism," policy of, 195.

Prussia (see Germany).

Public International Unions, 112:
Telegraphic Union, 112.
Universal Postal Union, 112.
International Union for the Pro-

tection of Industrial Property, etc., 113.
Metric Union, 113.
Agricultural Institute, 113.
International Maritime Office, 113.
Sugar Convention, 113.
Customs Tariff, 113.
Inter-Parliamentary Union, 113.
Bureau of Arbitration, 113.
great value of, 113.

Recognition of States, 61.
Reinsch, P. S., 103.
Religion, 25.
Resources, 36.
Revenues, 27.
Rights of States:
 "Declaration of Rights," 12, 56, 68.
 failure of International Law to define, 13.
 to independence, 13, 61, 62, 63, 64, 65.
 to equality, 13, 68.
 to existence, 14, 58, 60, 154.
 to sovereignty, 13, 64, 65, 66.
 no common conception of, 18, 218.
 confused with interests, 56.
 legal rights, 57.
 "inherent," "absolute," "primordial," "fundamental," 57, 72.
 nationalism basis of right to exist, 60.
 definition of required, 107.
 of aliens, 107.
Roberts, Earl, 155.
Roosevelt, President, 195.
Root, Mr. Elihu, 19, 57, 162.
Roumania, 49.
Russia, 28, 40, 51, 79, 88, 91, 92, 153, 208.
Russo-Japanese War, 130.

Salonica, 39.
Samoa, 91.
San Marino, 35.
Sanitary Board, 111.
Savarkar Arbitration, 89.
Secretaries of Embassies and Legations, 197.

Self-redress:
 abandonment of, 201.
 international, 52.
Serbia and the Serbs, 32, 38, 39, 84, 214.
Servitudes, 91.
Ships and Arms, 123.
Sicily, 28.
"*Sittlichkeit*," 50, 154.
Socialism, 28, 151.
South Africa, 63, 78.
Sovereignty:
 corollary of right to exist, 64.
 origin of term, 64.
 synonymous with independence, 65.
 absurd in application, 65.
 theory of no real value, 66.
Spain, 78, 215.
Spanish-American War, 78.
Spinoza, 49.
Spitzbergen, 109.
State, The:
 origin and nature of, 23.
 definition of, 23.
 community of interests the basis of, 24.
 ethical justification of, 30.
 physical essentials of, 35.
  population, 35.
  territory, 36.
  variety of resources, 36.
  economic defense, 37.
  rivers, ports, 37.
  "hinterland" doctrine, 38.
  adjacent islands, 39.
  free ports, 39.
  boundaries, 40.
 political essentials, 40.
  reciprocating will, 41.
  popular guarantees, 42.
  constitutions, 42.
  defects of American Constitution, 42.
  defects of German Constitution, 43.
 should be self-sufficient, 37, 54.
 moral personality of, 44.
 German theory of, 45, 46.
 Anglo-Saxon theory of, 45.
 distinction between individual and, 47, 48, 101.
 the security of, its supreme law, 49.

INDEX

the "conscience" of, 50, 52.
rights and interests of, 56.
independence of, 61, 62.
sovereignty of, 13, 65.

Status Quo, 59, 159.
Suez Canal, 109.
Suzerainty, 65.
Switzerland, 13, 29, 36, 62, 114.

Taft, President, 195.
Tangiers, 109.
Territory, 36.
Thomasius, 21.
Treaties:
  should be for brief periods, 42.
  Prussian valuation of, 218.
Trieste, 39, 211, 215.
Tripoli, 81.
Turkey (see Ottoman Empire).

United States:
  defective Constitution of, 43.
  neutrality of, 47.
  and Colombia, 51.
  and Cuba, 62.
  and Canada, 63.
  and Samoa, 91.
  complaint against Great Britain as the "arsenal of the Confederates," 120.
  complaint of Germany against, 122.
  and Napoleonic Wars, 128.
  and "The Great War," 129.
  Geneva Arbitration, 144.
  not the mediator of Europe, 147.
  military preparedness of, 156.
  failure of Pan-American policy, 160.
  assertion of hegemony by, 161.
  conflicts of laws in, 167.
  duty toward Pan-American nations, 172.
  foreign relations, 181.
  and France, 185.
  Diplomatic Service, 191, 196.
  Monroe Doctrine a permanent policy of, 195.

Venezuelan Preferential Claims Arbitration, 88.

War:
  causes of, 76, 94, 206.
  Spanish-American, 78.
  South African, 78.
  Russo-Japanese, 79.
  Italo-Turkish, 81.
  Balkan, 82.
  "The Great War," 84.
  scientific treatment of causes, 86.
  substitution of law for, 173, 201.
War ("The Great War"), 1, 15, 32, 34, 49, 84, 93, 129, 140, 146, 153, 174, 205, 214, 218.
War of 1812, 128.
Washington (President), 185.
Westlake, 135.
Wheaton, 65.
World Peace, 172.

Rebound MAR 1 9 '43